Neighborhood Stories

By Larry Brasen Sr.

Published by Dry Heat Publishing, LLC   Payson, Arizona 85541

ISBN 978-163795660-1

ISBN 978-163795660-1

Neighborhood Stories

3

Larry Brasen Sr.

Table of Contents

Scobey, Montana

A Great place to get started!

Short Pants and Hightop Shoes

THE RANT: This rant started out because of my mother.

Every time I see a guy wearing Bermuda Shorts I just try to avert my eyes. How ugly can a pair of legs from above the knees and down to the ankles be? I mean, Good Grief. Didn't you ever grow up? Holy Cow! UGLY!!! I know I'm causing some people to be utterly pained with my statement. But how can I help it? Oh, by the way, for those of you who practice Political Correctness, can you get over it? I mean, Good Lord! No growing up for you.

And what about those terrible Tee-Shirts? I mean, you've been there, saw that, got the Tee-shirt. That doesn't mean you HAVE to WEAR the miserable thing! Those flabby or skinny arms poking out of the things they call armholes have got to be the ultimate in Ugly. Get out of kindergarten and put on real clothes. Pants that cover your hopeless shins. Shirts with arms that cover your bald flabbed out elbows.

And how about those Tennis Shoes. How plebeian can you get? I mean, come on man. Try on a pair of grown up shoes. You don't have to do tassels. You can do laces if you have to. But tennis shoes? Oh yeah, you're going down in the history of fashion flops big time. I saw a guy wearing tennis shoes with a tuxedo. Or how about the guy I saw on TV hiking in the desert in Bermuda Shorts, Knee socks and flip flops. You just can't do that.

<u>This is how the "Rant" got started.</u>

When I was a little kid, before going to First Grade (There was no kindergarten in 1945 in Scobey), the very height of fashion was to dress your little boy in Shorts with a bib, a short sleeved shirt, socks that came up to your shins and what I call high top brown leather lace up shoes. It was obligatory to have your little boy dressed in this fashion. If you appeared in public dressed otherwise, you as the mother could possibly face shunning on Sunday at the Lutheran Church. (Not really) Even at the age of five years, I had a real sense of wanting to be able to finally wear long pants in public during the summer. Oh My, My, My!!! How I hated to look down at my little chicken legs sticking out of those accursed short pants. Please God, let me just skip five and move directly to six with long pants and long sleeved shirts. But God and time both move excruciatingly slowly when you are dreading the wearing of Horrible clothes.

"Oh, Larry, don't you look just great. Are you looking forward to visiting the Ice Cream Bar down town. (Since the men in town had their Bars in which to hang out, the nicer Ladies had their Ice Cream Bar as opposed to a parlor.) What do you think you'll be getting? Maybe a milkshake or a sundae?" encouraged Mom.

I was just thinking about sitting in that booth we always sit in and not being the right size to eat my ice cream or milk shake. At five years of age you're at the wrong size for just about everything. If I got up on my knees on the bench, then I could at least spoon the ice cream into my mouth. I had better not order a milk shake. They came in that glass with a pedestal for a base and then blossomed up and out into a three inch opening at the top. If I sat on my knees, I would still be too short to fit the straw into the glass. I would have to take it down from the table and hold it in my lap and the last time I did that it spilled. Well, we had to walk all the way down town because mom didn't know how to drive. I could think about it on our way.

Scobey is subject to just about every kind of weather condition imaginable. The "Old Timers" say, "If you don't like the weather just wait five minutes." It'll change that quickly. This was one of the hottest days we had seen all summer. We had been down town for the Fourth of July with the parade and everything. That had been over a month before and it had been hot. This was almost damp and hot.

We started walking North on the path (the streets were dirt and there were no sidewalks) in front of our house. Then we turned West at Gendrue's home and headed toward the Catholic Church. A couple blocks later we hit Main Street. There seemed to me to be a lot of traffic on Main. I turned to mom and asked, "Is something special happening?" To which she replied, "Well, Larry, we'll just have to wait and see, won't we?"

We walked down Main Street to the Rex Theater where we crossed over the street to the Gorham Hotel and then North again til we got to the Ice Cream Bar. Two guys were in a booth and they got up and offered the booth to mom and me. I thought that was really nice. Mom sat down on one side and I clambered up on the other. They didn't have a waitress so the lady behind the counter had to come over and take our order. The place was full of people. Everybody was talking but almost in whispers. I couldn't help but feel like something unusual was happening but I had no idea what it was. Everyone would look out of the window onto the street and then start talking in those strange muted voices. Mom ordered a Cherry Phosphate and I had a Chocolate Sundae. Just as we were finishing our Ice Cream a strange sound started on the street. Then I realized what it was. It was the fire siren. But people had surged out onto the middle of the street. Someone started honking their car horn. Then two...then more...then all...the people started yelling at the top of their voices. All the church bells in town started ringing. People started dancing in the street.

Everyone was hugging each other and laughing and crying. Outright sobbing…

Mother said to me, "Larry. This is special. The war is over. We won. Try to remember this day, what we did, what we heard, what we saw. This is History!"

At five I didn't understand what it all meant, but I'll never forget that afternoon on the Main Street of a dusty little country town in Northeastern Montana when I no longer really cared about Short Pants and High Top Shoes.

THE TWENTY DOLLAR BILL

Summer time in Scobey, Montana in 1947 was about as good as life could get. It was get up bright and early, (no clock) hungry. I loved our cereal. It came in great boxes. I was old enough to read and boy, did the boxes have readability. The big old Shredded Wheat that didn't even fit into the bowl had separator stiff paper dividers with Indian Scout stuff to learn about and in case you had been invaded by some unknown species of wild animal in the night, you could learn what their footprints looked like. Wheaties was the breakfast of CHAMPIONS!!! (If you ate Wheaties, you became a Champ.) Rice Krispies had the Snap, Crackle and Pop triplets. Man oh man, you could really hear them talk to you until it all went soft. Cheerios were magic O's. No tellin' what could happen if you ingested a few of them. Put the carbohydrate laden stuff in a bowl, pour on the milk, ladle on several teaspoons of sugar and Wow! You were set for the day. (Our Federal Government even told you how the Carbs were needed to form the basis of the food Pyramid). And you could send away for really nifty stuff like the Master Decoder Ring, the spring loaded airplane that could fly right off your finger, and assorted things like comic books in miniature, Magic words of Poof Poof Piffles, Make me just as small as Sniffles. (That was Mary Jane and Sniffles for those of you who don't remember.)

After breakfast there was always the garbage if it needed to be emptied. I was so excited when I got to be old enough to burn the garbage. I got to carry a book of matches with me out to the garbage and actually light it on fire. We had our garbage cans, two of them out in the alley. We all burned our garbage daily. (Not a very pleasant smell.) Some days it would burn hot and sometimes it would just kind of smolder. Then one of the chores I had to do was weed the garden. A row a day keeps the weeds at bay. We had a large garden with veggies of all sorts. I loved to eat carrots right out of the ground. Just wipe 'em off with your dirty hands, wipe on your jeans, and eat them fresh, dirt and all. Another favorite of mine were little ol' green peas. When the peas inside the pod were about half the size of the eraser on the yellow pencil, just pop 'em in your mouth and it was an explosion of pure sugar in each pea. (Still love it today).

Then it was time to whistle up my next door friend, Alden. We had been to a matinee serial at the old Rex Theater where the Little Rascals (I think) whistled up their friends with a form of a Whippoorwill tweet. It couldn't be heard for very great distances but we were right next door to each other. He and his brother Clive were probably in their garden, doing their chores so we were basically next to each other. Tweetle-ee tweee...Tweetle-ee tweee… Tweetle-ee Tweee. (Always had to do it three times like that. Anyone else horning in on our secret whistle would be spotted immediately because they didn't know the secret three.)

"Hey, whatcha up to today? Anything?" I asked.

"Nah. Just weedin'." Alden said.

I said, "Well, I'm just about done over here. How about you?"

"Yeah, pretty close." was his reply.

"What do you say we slip up and down some alleys and pick up some pop bottles?"

That was one of our favorite things to do. Pop bottles had a three cent rebate on them. If you got a sixteen ounce one you got a nickle. We went up and down alleys with my radio flyer red wagon with the black handle and collected bottles. Sometimes one of us would ride in the wagon while the others would push and just see how fast you could go. Since none of our streets were paved (except the highway through town) it would be assumed that the alleys were dirt. That was where everyone put their 55 gallon oil barrels they used for garbage. Sometimes we would stop at a particularly well groomed garden and pull a carrot or two. It was on this exact day that the unexpected happened.

As I was pulling the wagon on the side of the alley where the weeds grew the thickest, I noticed what looked like a dollar bill in among the dead and decaying leaves on the ground. I stopped and said the obligatory, "Dibs on the money!" I freed it from the weeds and wonder of wonders, I discovered a Twenty Dollar Bill in my hand. That was the most money I had ever held in my hands. I sat down on the wagon in a trance.

Alden said, "Let me see it!"

I said, "Here, look! No touching!"

"Whatcha gonna do with it?" from Alden.

"I don't know. I suppose somebody lost it back here. Maybe we should look around and see if there is any more."

"You know what? I'm gonna go over to the police station. It's right next to the Grocery store. I'll find out if somebody reported it missing. We can turn the bottles in at the store while we're there and get our money."

At the sheriff's office we were greeted with, "Well now, what can we do for you lads today?"

I said, "We were hunting for bottles when I found this twenty dollar bill. I just wondered if anybody reported missing one today." I showed him the bill.

He reached out and took the bill from me and made a very thorough examination of it. "No, I can't say that anyone has reported it missing today. If you want to I can keep it for you here in case some one shows up."

I said, "I guess that would be the right thing to do. If nobody claims it, then it'll be mine?"

"Yes, I suppose so," He said.

With that Alden and I went to the store, got our bottle money and went home for a well deserved lunch.

Dad happened to be home for lunch that day. As mom put sandwiches, soup and milk on the table and dad came to sit down, I said, "Guess what?"

I guess grownups sometimes don't like playing the *guess what* game because dad said, "What?"

I told them both about finding the twenty dollar bill and giving it to the sheriff down town to which dad said, "You did what?"

I repeated my story in a little more detail and dad started shaking his head, first back and forth and then up and down. I didn't see him act that way very much so I said, "Is something wrong?"

Dad said, "Hurry up with your lunch. We're going to go downtown and get your twenty dollar bill back right away, McGee." He called me McGee after the radio show character Fibber McGee and Molly.

At the sheriff's office we walked in and the man with my twenty dollar bill stood right up and said, "Good afternoon, Francis. I was hoping I'd see you here."

Dad said, "My son here says he found a twenty dollar bill and you took it to see if you could find the rightful owner. I think you and I both know who the rightful owner is. I just came down to see that the rightful owner gets it back right now."

"Absolutely!"

I don't remember what the twenty dollars bought but whatever it was couldn't have been worth what I thought of my dad that day. I don't suppose he remembered it for long but I SURE DID!!!

My Second Grade

Since my birthday falls on the Ides of March, I started
First Grade in the fall of 1946 when I was six years old.
All I can remember of the first grade is feeling nice
about going to school. It was really kind of a no-pressure
school year. The most complex task I remember was the
coloring of a handout picture of a dog, dog house, a boy
and a girl jumping rope. This was taking place on a
parent visitation day so everyone was on their best
behavior. There was the name of a color on each of the
objects and the students each had the requisite box of
crayolas handy. Of course I could read the words brown,
green, yellow and red. Of course I knew the names of the
colors in the box. Of course it just never occurred to me
that I was supposed to color the objects the labeled color.
My dog was green! I was having a GREAT time! My
blue sky was a sort of lavender! I was feeling
WONDERFUL! I didn't notice the puzzled looks on the
faces of the parents and their shaking heads as they
passed my desk where I was so busily employed. "Were
you supposed to color the dog brown?" my mom
whispered, leaning down close to my ear. It all came
clear. I had done a horrible job interpreting the lack of
instruction that had accompanied the handout. (I am sure
I just wasn't paying attention when the teacher, Mrs.
Thompson, handed it out. I like to refer to this condition

as <u>Marching to the beat of my own drummer.</u> (Many years later it was referred to as A.D.D.)

Second grade started out as a continuation of First grade. Mrs. Morrison, my teacher was another quite nice lady who was a substitute mother and instructor. I remember I particularly liked a little girl named Jane. I thought she was as nifty as could be. Part of what made her so attractive was the way she acted so superior to me. On the other hand, the little girl named Donna, who's nose seemed to run most of the time, was uncontrollable attracted to me. At recess I would try my best to station myself near Jane as she jumped rope with a couple of other girls. Her stocking-ed legs seeming to magically appear from beneath her neatly pressed little dress. If I ever caught her looking my way I would be extremely busy looking at my shoe. In the meantime Donna was never far away. It was, "Hiii, Larrrry!", with an incredible smile and a come-hither look in her eye as she sniffed her way to my side. That would send me to the "Jungle Gym" where I could finally climb high enough to get away from her.

Dad was a wheat farmer. Hard, Red Spring Wheat. Plant in the spring, summer fallow in the summer, harvest in the fall and then go to work for one of the implement shops in town doing mechanic work on farm equipment to supplement the farm income which often wasn't enough to make it through the winter. As he was finishing up the farm work for the year in mid-October,

the Elementary School was putting on what they referred
to as a play. I'm not sure what the theme of the play was
but I think it was some sort of historical drama written
by one of the parents in conjunction with the teaching
staff. The whole Elementary School was involved and I
got to play the part of the Indian Chief "Rain-in-the-
Face". Mom had been feeling "poorly" (Mom was from
Southern Indiana, "Poorly" was a comment they used to
indicate one didn't feel up to snuff, but was well enough
to be out of bed and about one's daily chores), as the fall
approached but she managed to make my Indian Chief
costume including a wonderful war bonnet. It was my
initial role to play on stage. Mom told me, "Now, Larry,
when you're on the stage you have to exaggerate
everything you do. Every action you take, you have to do
bigger. Every sound you make, you have to do louder.
When you're talking to someone on stage with you,
glance to the end of the gym and yell loud enough to be
clearly heard way back there." I took her at her word.
Man oh man did I dance around that "Camp Fire". Knees
all the way up to my chest and stomp down hard. When I
"Hi-yi-yied" you better believe you could hear it all the
way in the back. When it came time for the curtain call I
strode on stage, the audience went wild for me and I
bowed deeply and thought, "THANK YOU VERY
MUCH." I'm afraid I've been bitten by that bug ever
since.

Mom's older sister, Thelma, lived with her husband and family in Minneapolis, Minnesota. Through the exchange of letters mom and Thelma had arranged to make an appointment for mom, with a medical specialist in the Twin Cities. As soon as the play was done dad bundled us up and took us to Wolf Point, Montana where he deposited us, Mom, Joanne, age 3 and Me age 7 on the Empire Builder and we headed East. We left our older brother, Don, in Scobey, with Dad, so not to miss school. We were supposed to be gone for no more than two weeks.

I might take a couple seconds here to mention that in the year 1947 the telephone was used for long distance calls only in dire emergencies such as a death in the family. The great American Highway System was a glint in "Ike's" eye. Top speed on those old roads was between 35 and 50 miles an hour. (50 only if a life depended on it) Air travel was unheard of. The quickest news could be heard on the radio. Reporters were pretty unbiased. (Sort of like Joe Friday, "The facts ma'm, just the facts.") News reels were shown at the local movie theater. That was about 10 minutes of pictorial presentations with great fan-fare from all over the world featuring men with those deep, commanding voices telling us what we were seeing. Family entertainment was Saturday night in a semi-circle on the floor in front of the radio listening to some of the famous broadcasts like "Fibber Mcgee and Molly","The Jack Benny Show", and <u>"The Shadow"</u>,on the clear channel stations like KXEL at 1540 AM out of "WATALOO, IOWAA". That family time came after the kids took their weekly baths in the living room in a wash tub filled with water heated on the kitchen stove. Last thing on Saturday night was the reading of the Sunday Comics out of the New York Tribune which dad had on order at the local Rexall Drug Store. Long distance travel was the domain of the Rail Road. And the Rail Road took the ultimate pride in the service it provided. Stations were beautiful, clean, modern, and had the travelers interests foremost in their planning. Depots were true works of art themselves. The train companies spared no expense to insure the customers were well taken care of.

We brought our own brown bag of sandwiches and fruit to eat on the trip there. We didn't have a Pullman suite, but rather we sat on the bench seats in the passenger car. I remember actually getting to go to the Diner Car for lunch. Mom said to me, "Larry, let's just order that Chicken Ala King and share it." I wanted to know what Chicken Ala King was. Mom said, "That means it is Chicken that is so good that even a king would order it."

I was impressed! A KING!! When I got a chance to taste a little bite of it, I was more impressed. I held that dish in high esteem for years. Mom would say, "Let's have Chicken Ala King", and that was enough to get me to the table "pronto". I confess I still like it almost as much as it's big brother, BLT and BLT's bigger brother, Welsh Rarebit. I guess I'm just a sucker for toast.

MINNEAPOLIS

Aunt Thelma lived with her husband Archie Williamson and their two girls Roberta and Diane. Their home was large. Back home in Scobey, we would have said, "Oh, I suppose the banker must live here." But in the city all the houses looked the same. Lawns, shrubbery, flowers beds, sidewalks, paved streets, garages for the automobiles, little sheds for the yard equipment, homes made of bricks with large windows to let in the light. Inside was more of the same. Uncle Archie had to go to work every morning at a job where he called himself an Engineer. I was disappointed to find it had nothing to do with my new fascination, Rail Roads. He had to work on stuff he called Blue Prints. Thelma was a homemaker. She also was a wordsmith, writing stories and poems. Roberta and Diane were enough older than me to make them not very interesting to me. We had our own bed room. Very neat and it smelled like a lady.

Our first full day was planned out so the ladies could go "Shopping". To me it seemed like there was a lot more "looking" than "Shopping". There was the trying on of clothes of all sorts and just generally being swept up with all the big city had to offer. The largest town we had ever been in was Missoula, Montana witch was quite large by Scobey standards. THIS city was filled with the stuff you couldn't even dream about.

As the day wore on I started really feeling the strain of the time on the train. I just got more and more tired as the ladies shopped to their hearts delights. I noticed I was feeling warm. The room seemed to change its appearance every time my heart beat. In the clothing section of the Department Store we were in I stopped in front of a three way mirror with a little step in front of it. I felt so tired that I sat down on the step. All I know is that before long mom was waking me up with a rather strong shaking saying, "Larry, Larry are you all right?"

"I'm just real tired, mom,"I said. I fought to keep my eyes focused. I faded away.

HOSPITAL

I awoke later. How much later I don't know. I do know it wasn't the same day. I do know it wasn't a familiar room. I do know it wasn't a familiar bed. And I do know it wasn't a familiar lady in a white uniform with a big old needle in her hand. I tried to formulate a question. Nothing worked correctly.
"Well, my fine little friend, How are we today?" She intoned in a voice that said she said that in exactly the same way to everyone she woke up that was unable to answer.

I answered, "Uhhh".

Sounding a little more friendly, she said, "There, There. You haven't had a drink of water for some time now. I'll just get you an ice cube to suck on. That'll help get that voice working a little better." She dug an ice cube out of a pitcher of water at the bedside and popped it into my mouth. When I tried to swallow the moisture came right up through my nose. I was alarmed. Wiping my face, she said, "Don't worry. That happens all the time. There, How's that now?"

Then came the part I was not looking forward to. "Well, now. If you'll just roll over a little, I'll give you this shot in your hip." I tried to follow her instruction, but there was just not any roll in my little body. I said, "Uhhh", while shaking my head.

"Well, now. Let's just see if we can give you a little roll with my help. Here we go. Okay, now. Are you ready for your shot?"

Once again I said what had become my favorite word, "Uhhh!"

At that point I felt the needle sink into my butt. "Hey! Ouch!"

Turning towards the door she said, "There, There now. That wasn't so bad, was it?" She left the room before I said the obligatory words, "Uhhh, uhhh."

I didn't know I had been whisked away from the department store where I had passed out to the ER at the hospital. Once there the emergency team was unable to diagnose my condition so out of an abundance of caution, they placed me in a quarantine room on the third floor. I also didn't remember that I had been drifting in and out of consciousness for 3 days. I have no idea how they diagnosed Typhoid Fever. Since this was before the wide use of antibiotics they were shooting me in the butt (HIP my butt) every 2 hours with something called a Sulfa Drug. The needle was long and had a heck of a diameter. It hurt. What I also didn't realize was that the authorities had quarantined Archie and Thelma's home with my mom and sister and all the Williamsons inside. I'm sure I'll never know Archie's reaction to not being allowed to go to work. I suppose he could do some of the work at home. Little did I know that hospital room would be my existence for the next 8 weeks.

<u>What follows is any and probably all of my memories of my time in the hospital.</u>

First of all, I must say that since this all happened when I was seven and I'm writing this shortly after my eightieth birthday, don't trust this to be an exact report of what happened. It is rather a memory that has become compacted in one extremely small brain cell somewhere up there. Hopefully I can convey what I *feel* about what I remember of the experience.

In answer to the question of I.V.s, I don't know if I had any or not. I imagine I did. How I was taken care of concerning bodily elimination, once again, my brain has (thankfully) shut that all out. I do seem to remember eating a lot of soup, crackers, Jello, and soft stuff. Since my mom and sister were quarantined in my aunt's house, I didn't get to see anyone I knew.

My room was located on one of the upper floors, I believe the third or maybe the fourth. I had a wonderful view of the street in front of the hospital. I spent a lot of time watching cars and people coming and going down below. The sidewalk at night looked like a scene from a Film Noir Movie. There were street lights casting pools of light on the sidewalk. Some trees obscured the view in places. Sometimes at night I would watch people walking on the sidewalk appear and disappear from one pool of light to the next and from tree to tree. It stirred my imagination.

Part of the schedule was my every two hour shot in the hip (butt). At first the nice nurse would say, "Okay, let's see here. Which side did you get this last time?" After a while I told her, "Just go ahead and shoot it wherever you like. It doesn't make any difference to me any more."

My nurse was wisely concerned about my mental inaction. She taught me a game of solitaire I could play holding the cards in my hands. It had to do with matching suits and matching nominations. Your score at the end was the number of cards you still held in your hand. (An easy solitaire I still sometimes play today when I'm away from my computer.)

I'm sure they brought me reading material, but I have no recollection of what it was. I did enjoy a new gift of a tube of plastic goop. (Had a strong odor.) It came with a small hollow straw. The object was to place a glob of the goop on the end of the straw, making sure it was secure. Then blow in the straw until the goop at the end of the straw formed a bubble. When you carefully removed the bubble from the straw, sealing the hole, you had a bubble that could last for some time.

After a time I was able to sit up. I didn't realize that the longer I stayed in bed, the more my legs began to atrophy. One day a few weeks into my isolation I thought about standing up in bed. As soon as my nurse had made her stop to see me I decided to give standing up in bed a try. I was surprised and alarmed that all my legs did was shake. Holding on to the bedstead, I tried to stand. No Go! I sank down on the bed and thought about my situation. I slept on it.

The next day, after breakfast, when I knew I wouldn't be interrupted, I tried walking on my knees the length of the bed and back. It wasn't easy but I got the job done. I did that two more times that day, scuttling under the covers at the least sound of anyone outside my door. Continuing that procedure for several days, until it got easy to do, I determined to try standing on the bed again. Still a little shaky but able to maintain for a minute or two, I knew I was on the right course of action. Within days I was walking on the bed, head to foot and back.

Soon I was walking on the floor around the room. I never told anyone about my extra curricular activities.

After a time the quarantine at the Williamson house was lifted and my personal infectiousness was gone my mom got to visit me. That was really nice. I knew I would be leaving the hospital soon. One night I woke out of a sound sleep. It was as though I heard something in the room with me. I looked around the room as well as I could. The only light was coming in from outside the window. After determining I was alone, I glanced out the window. Stories below me was the light-pooled sidewalk. Someone was walking away from the front door. As he passed through the first pool of light I realized it was my dad. What was he doing here? Why? How? He stopped at the center of the second pool of light and looked right straight up at me. "DAD! I'm right up here!", I yelled. Shaking his head and replacing his ever present hat, he walked, slump-shouldered, away.

Never in my life had I ever suffered such a profound sense of loss. My breath caught in my chest. My eyes filled with tears. Never in my life had I ever conceived of losing my father. I looked again and there was no one. Frantic, I searched up and down the sidewalk, looking for any last glimpse---any car moving---anything at all.

Release Day! By golly, everybody crowded into my room. Archie, Thelma, Roberta, Diane, Mom, Dad came, Joanne and even Don. My main nurse and 2 doctors were there. People were picking up all kinds of stuff including my pack of cards and getting everything ready to go. There was a wheel chair…,"I can walk," I said.

"Oh, no, no, no. You just don't know how weak your legs are from all the bed rest you've had", the nurse said. "Here, let me help you into the chair. Besides, Its hospital policy. All patients must be wheeled out of the front door to waiting vehicles."

"Oh", I said. "Okay." With that I allowed them to help me to the chair.

Outside the sun was bright. The sky had never seemed that blue. The clouds puffing along had never seemed so fluffy. We got to the thick glass door and when we stopped for them to open it for us, I proudly stood up. I strode through the door and bowing said,"THANK YOU VERY MUCH!"

Much to everyone's surprise I strolled to the door of the waiting car and to the cheering of all I moved on to the rest of my life.

<u>BACK IN SCOBEY</u>

After an extended period of rehab at home during which mom got my assignments from school and conducted home schooling, I finally got to get back to my Second Grade Class. Mrs. Morrison and the kids were glad to see me back. I had checked around for Jane and found her across the room in a group of girls. I thought, "If she looks at me, I'm gonna look right back at her!" I didn't have to be too concerned because sure enough here came Donna, sniffing over. "Hi Larry, are you all (sniff) right?". "Yup, all right! You?", I replied. I guessed everything was back to normal.

The folks had to answer a lot of questions earlier to the doctors in Minnesota. They wanted to know how I could have contracted typhoid and no one else had in our little town. When they heard that we had our milk delivered twice a week they asked about the sanitary conditions at the dairy. They asked if the milk was pasteurized and of course it wasn't. They said that it was possible the milk could have been contaminated at the point it was bottled. There was no consensus about the cause.

When we got back, Dad bought a cow. There was a little barn shelter on a fenced lot a couple of blocks South of our house next to the water tower he could rent and he milked the cow daily, bringing the milk back home. He purchased a home pasteurizing machine and we never had to worry again about our milk supply. I enjoyed going "Milking" with him. I was very interested in the whole procedure. He had a little stool hanging on the side of the milking stall that he would set in just the right place and then putting the milk bucket under the cow he would sit milking. At first the cow would slap her tail at dad and he would get a little irritated. Finally he solved the problem by tying a piece of twine to the stall and then the other end around the end of the cows tail. Problem solved. I was impressed.

Nothing could have prepared me for what happened on what I called the BIG DAY. Dad and I walked to the little barn yard and he started the milking program...Cow in place...Stool in place...Pail in place...Tail in place...Pail about half full...The cow lifted her hind foot and placed it squarely in the pail. Milk all over...Dad jumped up and shouted, "You Son Of A Bitch…" (I had never heard him say that before.) He walked right up in front of the cow...doubled up the fist of his right hand hit that cow with all his might right between the eyes. The cow's front legs immediately buckled and down on the bed of hay she went. WOW!!! After that, she never gave dad a bit of trouble again for as long as he had her. I decided then and there to NEVER mess around with Dad's pail!

I was only back to my class for a few weeks when I came down with another illness. We had no doctor for the town at the time so people had to make do on their own. Already weakened by my previous illness I was in bed right away. All I can remember was that both my legs were getting stiff and hurting like crazy in the joints. The muscles and joints were totally tensed to a point that my legs lay straight out in front of me on the bed. I couldn't move them or my feet.

I don't know how Esther Gulickson, a nurse, found out about my condition, but she paid a visit to our home.

After an exam she said, "Larry, I am going to have to get your ankles and knees and hips working again. This could hurt quite a bit. Do you think you could be big enough and brave enough to help me with this?"

I thought about all the shots I had taken and I promptly replied, "Okay".

She carefully took my left foot in hand and began bending it toward my shin. It took my breath away. She moved it back and forth many times and it fought the movement all the way. She then took my lower leg and bent it at the knee, working it the same way. Then she flexed my thigh to work the hip joint the same way. Each of these hurt more than the previous one. Then she repeated the entire process on the right leg. I knew that I had told her I could be BIG and BRAVE but the pain caused tears to come to my eyes. I didn't scream...I didn't cry...but I'm pretty sure there were whimpering and groaning sounds filling the house. Esther came to the house every day until she was no longer needed. When we did finally get a doctor in town, mom described the symptoms I had experienced. He said that in all likelihood I had contracted a case of the dreaded polio. He said that Esther had probably saved me from being crippled by the disease. How did she know what to do? What led her to do what was probably not taught in any medical training. Something in the back of her mind must have conceived of the treatment. Like a bolt out of the Blue.

Between you and me, looking back on it, I happen to believe God sent Esther to me and touched her brain, telling her what to do. Living as long as I have and having suffered physical and emotional setbacks as everyone does, I say I would have to be a FOOL not to believe in Divine Intervention and Protection.
And THANK YOU ESTHER GULICKSON!!!

<u>BACK TO SCHOOL E.O.Y.</u>

On the first day back to school there were only a few days left until summer vacation. In Mrs. Morrison's Second Grade Class she conducted a game that I now call Geographic Sit Down. We had maps that were stored above the chalk board on rollups. The first two students in the first row stepped up to the map of the world, one on either side. Mrs. M would call out the name of a country and the first one to point to it with his finger got to remain at the map, while the loser sat down. Then the next one got up and the game continued. I was about the fifth one to get up. I sat down everyone in the class. FUN!!!

There was quite a discussion with the authorities, the teacher, and Mom and Dad, as to whether or not I should be made to repeat the Second Grade. Since I had missed nearly the entire year, it was a big question. They decided to give me an exam for the end of the year and allow the grade I got on it make the decision. So I took the test. I passed with flying colors. I had been home schooled by the Salutatorian of her graduating class! No Problem!!!

I thought to myself, "THANK YOU VERY MUCH!"

OUR APPLE TREE GANG

It was the fall of 1948. The spring had been merciful to the apple trees in Scobey. Usually the Spring weather coaxed the few apple trees we had in the town to bloom early. That was always a sign of great things to come. We kids couldn't wait for the great days of summer and then the post garden obligatory digging of caves where the garden had been just days before. If it hadn't been for school, Fall would have been my favorite season. The problem for apple trees in Scobey was that after the early bloom there almost always came the killing frost for two and three-quarter days, insuring that the apples would need to wait another year to complete their natural cycle. Yup!!! No apples again this year. There had been no murderous frost last spring so the apple tree on the alley across from John Brenden's yard was loaded. We figured that the witch that lived there (I have forgotten her name) had cast a spell on the weather to insure the apple crop would be bountiful. We knew she was a witch because we saw her using her broom to sweep off her back porch more than once. We didn't know if she could ride it or not but she was a witch none the less and to be greatly feared!

John's parents had a great yard for kids to play in. The lawn was large enough so we could have a bad-mitten court or a large croquette court and still have room left over. One other thing we really liked about John's yard was the lilac bushes around his house. They had been there long enough for them to reach at least six or seven feet in height and to come out away from the house several feet. By this time in the early fall we had kind of burrowed our way through the bushes in a way that left no trail and then formed a room against the house that was big enough to house several of us.

Our gang included the following boys: John, the boy whose parents owned the place, Alden and Clive who lived next door to me, David, who was the son of the Lutheran Minister, and Me. Alden and Clive were Catholics but that didn't bother us Lutherans because we knew we were going to Heaven and they just had to take their chances with what their parents were. Besides, we got Ludefisk and Lefsa once a year and they had to eat fish on Fridays.

Part of the Brenden yard was given over to an area of dirt where we could play trucks, cars, construction, and roads. When we weren't working on the construction of roads and abodes we would work at being good guys and bad guys. "You two be the bad guys today."

"Awe, we had to be the bad guys last time. I want to be the sheriff."

"You can't be the sheriff, you don't even go to the right church."

"That's not fair. Church don't count in sheriffs."

And sooo it goes…

But today was going to be totally different. A day that would live in INFAMY. From inside our bushy hide away we laid our malevolent plot. "Have you looked at the witch's apples? They are ripe enough for eating."

John said, "Maybe we should go ask the witch if we could have a couple."

David said, "Yeah."

I said, "Well, I'm not really afraid of her, but if we rang her doorbell she might do away with us. Like Hansel and Gretel."

Alden said, "That's just a story. She doesn't scare me."

I said, "Okay. You go ring the door."

Alden replied, "Clive, You can do it."

Clive sniffing his nose as he did on occasion, "Nope, not me!"

I said, "Let's go over to the construction zone and pretend to be having a good time playing cars. In the meantime we can look over the tree and see if she is out or whatever."

Over we go. Scoping out the scene of the crime.

Back in the "Robbers Den" Alden said, "Did you notice how the fence is right up to the tree. The apples are right above the fence right there. If you reach up and grab the branch, you can stand on the fence and stuff your apples in your pockets."

"You know," I said, "Somebody should climb up the tree about half way as a lookout. In case the witch comes out with her broom, he can let us know to get out of there."

David said, "I'll do that job. I'll sneak over the fence and climb right up the trunk of the tree til I get about half way up. There's a branch right there I can sit on to keep watch."

So the plot was laid. We crawled out of our hidey-hole one at a time and proceeded to the alley just around the corner from the garage. From there we proceeded to crawl on our bellies across sticks, bits of glass, and any kind of junk you might expect to find in an alley in 1948. David got through the fence and did a really sneaky crawl up the trunk of the tree. (Probably 5 inches in diameter) Up he snuck. Up about six feet, maybe seven. The tree was quite a bit thinner there than it was at the base. He was at the branch he had described. We came out of the prone positions and crawled to the barbed wire fence. Alden went in first then me then John and last came Clive, the youngest. We started picking apples like there was no tomorrow. They were small cherry red apples we called Crab Apples. The first bite would send your taste buds awhirl. After that you could gobble down a lot easily. All of us were in, on, or around the tree when...You guessed it...Out came the witch, broom in hand, SCREAMING, "YOU KIDS GET OUT OF MY TREE!" With that, the broom she was carrying became a rifle. She cocked the rifle and the report of a BB gun came across the space between her back porch and the tree. Up in the tree we heard David cry out, "OUCH!!!" Boy oh boy. Did you ever see four kids scramble for the alley like the witch was after them. **"Ouch, Yipes, Hey, That hurts.**"

Back in the "Robbers Den" again we looked around and said, "Where's David?"

John said, "I saw him caught up high in the tree. He's still there and the Witch has him."

"What are we gonna do?"

I said, "I just wanna go home!"

Alden and Clive said the same.

John said, "I'm going to turn myself in. It's not fair. The Witch has David and we all are to blame. I'm going over there right now."

I ran home and hid in the bathroom. Nobody was home and was I scared. I stood in the bathroom, looking in the mirror saying, "Boy, oh boy, I'm not ever doing that again. **Never, never, never!**"

My brother Don, who I hadn't seen or heard came into the bathroom and said, "What is it that you're never gonna do again?"

Startled, I muttered something nonsensical and went into our bedroom. I wanted to crawl under the bed with the dust bunnies and grimy stuff but knew he would dig me out so I crept on top and just closed my eyes.

Some day I'm going to ask John what happened when he met the witch with David. I think enough time has passed so I can finally hear the rest of the story.

THE POPCORN FIASCO

Popcorn! Doesn't the very word bring memories to your mind of the fluffy, salty, buttered and aromatic delicacy. I like to eat it by the handful! I also really enjoy consuming it one special kernel at a time, making a deliberate dent in the bowl of the unchosen left behinds. Then after seeing each of the chunks of cloud respond to their fate, reaching in and choosing another lucky piece of mist to adorn my palate before being downed in the inevitable dark hole known as my esophagus. And then, when my bowl is beginning to assume a more correct shape, my mate, unknowingly asks if she can have a little more, as though my artistic endeavor was of no consequence. Of course I say, "Why of course dear." Pretending that the kernels left in my bowl were no more than just that. A bowl of uneaten, popped corn, awaiting their fate.

Our grand daughter was four years old. We were living in Scottsdale, AZ on what was known as "The Ranch". It was a beautiful one floor home with a Great Room which combined the living room with conversation pit fire place, dining room and kitchen all under a two story ceiling. It was a three bedroom, two bath delight of open construction. Holly and Sam, our grand son of 6 years, were visiting. What a delight! I decided to pop a big bowl of pop corn, of course. So I wrangled out a two quart covered stainless steel kettle, some vegetable oil, a couple tablespoons of butter, and some pop corn kernels and put the pan on the burner to warm up the oil and butter. Holly, who was never far behind, said, "Whatcha Doin, Grandpa?"

I answered, "I'm going to make a nice big batch of pop corn for us all to enjoy."

She asked, "Aren't you gonna use the Micro wave for that?"

"No," I answered. "I'm just using these pop corn kernels right here", showing her the jar of Colonel Redenbachers kernels.

Her eyes got really big, she reached for the jar, handed it back and at the top of her voice exclaimed, "Sam, Sam!!! You gotta come quick! Grandpa's making pop corn from **SCRATCH!!!**

Ahhh, And the smell of it. The irresistible aroma of it all. The thought of going to the theater and not having a huge sack, No not a sack, a Bucket of the stuff. "Could you give it one more shot of that butter." Man, I can't wait to get seated in one of those relaxing bucket seats to get started eating my popcorn. Betty likes Jordan Almonds almost as much as I like the Corn. We both have those 3 gallon containers of ice surrounded by a cup of Diet Pepsi. (Diet because we are on a diet, of course.) Four big slurps and all that is left is ice. One of these days, after the PLAGUE, when we return to the theater, I'm going to say, "NO ICE!" She'll be pouring that 4 gallon Diet Pepsi for hours.

I used to buy candy coated rods of licorice about two-thirds of and inch long and about as big around as two Number 2 Ticonderoga Pencil leads. I moved from them to the soft multi-colored packs of Dots. I remember, I loved the reds. Give me a RED and I'll give you all the lemon and lime and orange and black. For a while I started in on eating Old Black Crows. (Black Gummy Dots) That got old fast. And then there was Black Cow on a stick. That was another confectionery treat I was unable to pass up. You know, it was no wonder my teeth were so rotten.

1948—Scobey, Montana

Ah! But Pop Corn! So my mother, decided early on that because I was the shyest child anyone had ever seen, that it would be good for me if she could manufacture situations into which she could place me where I had to interact with people. All people. Everybody!!! More about Mom's motivations later. She figured out a way that I could go into business for myself. This would have the effect of forcing me to deal with a variety of folks I didn't know. Mom's friend, Mrs. Funk, had a Lady's Haberdashery on the West side of Main Street. I think her first name may have been Selma, but that memory has gathered a little patina so you may be able to help me out there. Mom's idea was what I refer to as the ***Great Popcorn Fiasco!*** She worked it out

that we could bring our card table down town in my
Radio Flyer Wagon, in front of Mrs. Funk's shop, run an
extension cord into the shop, set the pop corn popper on
the table, plug it in, ladle in a little lard, pour in the
required amount of pop corn kernels, and start turning
the stirring rod after placing the top on the popper. I
asked if my buddy Alden could share in the adventure
and mom gave me the okay on that. I was the stirrer and
it was also my job to dump the corn into a big bowl on
the table. We had small brown paper sandwich bags we
filled with popcorn and charged ten cents a bag. Alden,
in the meantime, was pouring lemonade into wax lined
paper cups and charging a nickle a cup.

As soon as the smell of the popping corn
permeated the air, the customers were people deep at our
little business place. Of course we had salt for the corn
so as soon as they started eating the popcorn they wanted
something to quench their thirst. Lemonade was just the
ticket. It was the perfect spot for a popcorn stand. We
were located about 1/3 of the block South of the main
business intersection of town. Two doors down to the
North was a bar. There was another one across the street.
The pool hall was a few steps away. We were roughly a
block North of the Rex Theater and across the street.
Around 2:20 PM we began to notice folks grabbing the
popcorn sacks and heading up the street to the South and
across the street towards the Rex Theater. We hadn't
taken into account the fact that the theater ran a matinee

at 2:30 on Saturday afternoon. We didn't give it another thought. All was right in Heaven and Earth and our business was going to make us wealthy beyond our wildest dreams.

At about 2:45 PM a big old man came up to our stand. He looked like he was about to explode. You know, that red face you get just before you blow your top! I could tell he hadn't been breathing as he should because one bluish blood vein stood way out on his forehead. Parking himself in front of the pop corn table he demanded, "And who's idea is it to be selling pop corn out on the street at this time on a Saturday afternoon?"

Being of sound mind, I said, "That would be my mom! She's right inside Mrs. Funk's shop."

"Well," the man blustered, "I'm the owner of the Rex Theater and you're popcorn is ruining my business. I'll just have to speak to your mother." And with that he disappeared into the Ladies stuff for sale.

We couldn't help hearing their discussion out on the sidewalk where we were located. In a minute or two he came out of the door saying, "I'm going over to the Sheriff's office and have him put an end to this." Across the street he went, ignoring the traffic as he strode. I could see him in the sheriff's office across the street, hands waving, feet stomping and fist banging on palm. I couldn't hear what was going on but I could imagine his big mouth flapping away. As he and the sheriff came out of the office door, Mom appeared at the door of the shop. She stepped over to Alden and me and said in a very quiet and calm voice, "Now, you just let me handle this."

"May I help you gentlemen?" Mom queried.

"As you can see, Sheriff, here's the proof. No sales permit, no compliance with ordinances, just set up and start business. Mrs. Brasen, you should know better than to do this like that."

Mom said, "I was just hoping the boys could make a little money and get to know what it's like to own their own business. Get a little taste of dealing with people they don't know and getting a feeling of earning their way to success. Was that wrong?"

The sheriff looked at the owner of the theater and said, "You can't possibly expect me to tell these kids who are under parental supervision that they can't do this, can you. For crying out loud, a few bags of popcorn aren't going to break you! Give them a break and get your show going."

About that time mom said, "Well, Larry and Alden, I think we should break this all up and head up the street to the Ice Cream Bar. What do you say?"

We both loved the Ice Cream Bar. We packed everything in my Red Radio Flyer Wagon and trundled up the street to the Ice Cream Bar, mom in tow. We did have enough pop corn left to make a nice big batch to listen to the **Lone Ranger, Rides Again** on the radio when we got home.

The "*Glass Bomb*"

When we were kids, we were absolutely fascinated with smoking. I mean we would try smoking anything that would burn. If it stood still and was dry, baby, we tried smoking it. Coffee in a paper straw, real tobacco rolled up in a sheet of notebook paper, dad's pipe, cigarettes we filtched from our dads, Bull Durham in the paper in the orange pack that came with the stuff, and weeds of every description as soon as they were old and weathered enough to light up, it all burned and we were excited about it. We imitated our heroes, our dads, brothers, our uncles, our cousins, our grandparents, movie stars, athletes, singers, instrumentalists, HECK, Everybody who was considered anybody smoked and we couldn't wait to be old enough to join in that all inclusive club. We knew it was wrong and that made it even more attractive. One of our favorite weeds to try to smoke was what we called pig weed. It didn't look like a pig but we thought maybe pigs would eat them if they got a chance. Heck, pigs might even smoke them if no humans were watching. (Thank you Gary Larson)

We smoked in the out house. Yes, that's right. Right in the middle of the town of Scobey, Montana, we had an old fashioned out house. (Most people did) We also had a Coal shed at the back of our property. Back in there you'd never get caught. In the fall of the year what had been the garden became a series of tunnels covered with boards and dirt making kids caves for a couple of weeks. Smoke, Smoke, Smoke, Smoke, Smoke!!! I should mention that we didn't inhale any of the smoke. Probably would have killed us.

The Daniels County Memorial Hospital was being built. The back yard was nothing but a vast field of five to six feet tall Pig Weeds. We built trails through the weeds and made strange rooms in the weeds. Have you ever been in a strong, cold wind in the fall when even being in the sun was no comfort? Then you turn a corner out of the wind and the sun hits you and you just feel so fine. That's what it was like to be in the Pig Weed Room. That's what it was like to be in the kids caves, out of the wind. Boy, talk about raw material for smoking in the field of pig weeds. Just find last year's stalk and cut it off at about 4 inches and light 'er up! And you have to hold it just so between your pointer and middle fingers. You might even hold up the V for Victory sign just like that English guy did.

Another place for great smoking was the ghost house across the street from us. It had been deserted for years and allowed to start the process of falling back into the ground from which it had come. Most of it's window panes were broken, but one or two were still complete. The putty holding the panes in place had long ago withered and become a part of history. When the wind blew (more than occasionally) it would shake the window panes. When we were outside looking at the window it appeared to have someone inside moving. I think now it was merely our own reflection in the shaking glass. "Hey!!! Look!!! Did you see that movement behind that window?" We thought it was the ghost of a long dead past resident. It became the Ghost House.

It was a two story house and when we got up the nerve, we knew how to gain entry. A fellow wouldn't necessarily want to do it all by himself, (with the ghost in there) but with the company of good friends, anything was possible. I don't remember the name of the family that had lived there but I think it may have be Gendrue. (Sp) Next door was the Kindzerski property and on the other side to the South lived an older man who was eventually found dead beside his house. (More ghost stuff) In order to get inside and bedazzle the ghost, we had to climb up on a gas tank in the back of the house and gain entrance through a window. We noticed the tank had some liquid in it. It was about half full. Alden had checked the handle and had found that the gas came right out of the spigot. Very handy to know!!!

It was during this time that we saw the movie starring Spencer Tracy, titled "Bad Day At Black Rock". During the movie the hero, Spencer Tracy, was fighting for his life and found himself backed up against a vehicle, maybe an old pickup or a WWII Jeep. He didn't have a gun but he used a tactic that we (Alden and I) found interesting. He took an empty wine bottle and getting under the truck, loosened the gas line, filling the bottle with gasoline. Then tore off a part of his shirt, stuffed it in the neck of the bottle. I had no idea what he was going to use that for. Imagine my surprise and delight when lighting the shirt on fire with a zippo lighter, he stood and threw the gas filled bottle with the flaming fuse at a small group of antagonists and it smashed spreading gas and fire over all of them. He was able to escape. WOW!!! Well, Alden and I knew that the haunted house across the street had that barrel half full of what we called White Gas. It had to be time to re-enact the exact moment of *arsonism*. (is that a word?)

The first thing Alden and I did was to take my Radio Flyer Wagon on a bottle search. We weren't looking for just any glass bottle, some mason jar or such. No, we wanted a long necked bottle we could stuff a cloth in the top. And it had to break when we threw it on the ground. It had to be big enough to contain a goodly amount of fuel. Regular pop bottles were too small. We needed the next size up. I imagine we were looking for something in the 32 ounce category. After finding a couple of Ginger Ale bottles of the correct description, getting some pieces of cloth, and matches, we descended on the Ghost House.

"Here, you hold the bottle under here and I'll turn the knob."

"Okay, just be ready to turn it off when I say so."

We filled the first bottle with the White Gas and shoved the piece of cloth into the neck. Smiling like the fine gangsters we had become and were about to become, we hid the bottle in my wagon, in a pile of rubbish we found that had belonged to the ghost.

"Where are we going to do this?"

"How about in our alley behind our house near the garbage cans?" I volunteered.

So we exited the ghost yard out the back in it's alley and then South to the regular street. Took a right then past our street past Pat and Muriel Horton's and down the alley to the right past the Nelson's place to the Catholic Church vacant lot. "This looks like a good spot. Right here close to our burn barrel," Alden said.

"We need something hard to throw the bottle against. It won't break just hitting the ground." I said.

"How about this brick?"

"Oh, Yeah."I smiled, nodding approval.

"Get that rag soaked up real good," Alden said.

"Don't you want to throw it? It's your garbage can." I asked.

"Naw, you go ahead."

"Okay. Light 'er up!"

"Get out of the way! Here goes!"

With that I threw the Spencer Tracy *"glass bomb"* against the brick at the base of the garbage can. The bottle broke into pieces spewing burning gas over both garbage cans and on the ground all around. There was an intake of air where it hit the brick and with an intense upward movement of flame of easily six feet, the heat that radiated out to us two kids was more than twenty of us could have imagined. The best thing we could think of to do was run away. We ran down the alley, behind the French's garage where we had a little hide out. When we calmed down I noticed my arm was slightly singed from the burning fuse/rag. "Wow! That really worked great."

"Yeah, and it was a lot hotter than it was in the movie."

"You know, I don't think I want to do it with the other bottle today." Alden said.

"Me neither!" I added.

"I'm gonna head on over home." I said.

"Yeah, me too!"

WHY I FISH

My life-long affair with angling started with my Dad, Francis Brasen, and me on the farm some twelve miles Northwest of Scobey, Montana when I was ten years old. Dad had arranged a special work day. We picked up Ted Hackman, a day laborer that my dad could depend on to do the work needed to complete some of the labor intensive jobs on the farm. He was waiting for us on Main Street, outside the Cozy Café. We were going to pick rocks. A stone boat was attached to the tractor by a chain triangle. Dad pointed the tractor toward the end of the strip, tied down the steering wheel and with the old WD9 International in its lowest gear, and the throttle set on the lowest possible setting, we all trudged up the strip, grabbed whatever sizable stones we could find and plunked them on the stone boat's platform. Whenever the tractor needed a directional correction dad would slip on over and jerk on the wheel a tad until everything looked okay. It was sweaty, thirsty, dirty, dusty, muscle busting work. Often I would find a stone, nearly half my weight, partly embedded in the soil. By the time I could dig it out and pick it up, the stone boat, sliding along on its runners, was nearly out of reach. Stumbling with the heavy stone in my hands, I would reach the stone boat and heave my load on top its relatives already on board. Acknowledging this accomplishment, Ted grinned, "Good job there young Larry. That was sure enough a big one."

We would stop for a 15 minute drink/smoke break at about ten in the morning. Both Dad and Ted would light up and enjoy a smoke. Dad used what he referred to as taylor-mades, Chesterfields. Ted rolled his own, using the white sack of Bull Durham and the cigarette papers that came in an orange wrapper with the tobacco. At my age, I couldn't wait till I would be able to really be one of the men, and light up also.

Then we would take a half hour at noon for lunch. Ted brought his own lunch consisting of a couple sandwiches and a piece of cheese with water. Mom put our lunch together, packing it in a cardboard box she saved from a Getchel's Grocery delivery. There was enough room for a thermos of coffee, a thermos of milk, at least four sandwiches, two tomatoes, and two hard boiled eggs. In 1950 we hadn't heard of zip lock bags or any of the fancy plastic sandwich containers, so she wrapped them in waxed paper. Sometimes she would send my favorite, bacon and fried egg sandwiches. By the time we got to eat them, they had been in the sun so long they felt and tasted like they just came off the stove. We had salt and pepper for the tomatoes and the eggs. It was always amazing how dirty the hard boiled eggs could get during the de-shelling process. I would think, "Gosh, am I really going to eat that?" (And I did.) For dessert Mom would pack in one or two penny tootsie rolls. By eating them slowly and sipping on the still cool milk I could create my own chocolate concoction.

Following lunch we would take a 15 minute break around 2:30 and then there was a wonderful stop at around 4:00 P.M. It was then that dad, on this particular day, said, "Well, we've caught quite a load of stones. What do you say we try our luck at a load of fish down at the river?"

There were several buildings on the farm. Some of them were granaries intended to hold harvested wheat or barley. One had been the original homestead home Mom and Dad had built out there on that dry land prairie. It had been moved from its original spot to the place it now occupied. With its bare two by four studded walls it had been used as a home, a granary, and a storage building. At this particular time, it was being used as an experimental electronic facility. Dad had created a propeller out of wood, attached it to a D.C. generator and positioned it on the rooftop. Two coated copper wires led down through a window to a group of 12 volt batteries hooked up in parallel. Since the wind blew nearly all the time, the batteries remained charged. We could use D.C. light bulbs as well as have unlimited radio reception. Otherwise, we would have to run the pickup to listen to the radio. If we listened without running the engine we would take the risk of running down the pickup's battery and not being able to start the old 43 Ford for the return to town. The propeller on the roof was not quite balanced, so as it turned it created a thumping sound that echoed through the building. The stronger the wind, the more rapid and loud the thumping.

It was to this building we went to gather our fishing equipment. There, in a corner, were several eight foot long pine 1 X 2's. A thick braided fishing line was attached to the upper end in four notches and secured with a knot. The twenty to thirty foot line was wrapped around the board and ended with a number 6 or number 4 bait hook. About a foot above the hook was a split shot sinker and about two or three feet above the sinker was a cork. Originally intended as a stopper for a thermos, this cork had been split half way along its length with a knife. After the line had been inserted, a "farmers match" had been wedged along the line to hold it in place.

We each grabbed a pole and using them as improvised walking sticks, scrambled down the 35 foot embankment to the lazy North Fork of the Poplar. Out on the rolling plains, this waterway never felt the urge to get excited or nervous. The water slowly rounded each bend, trying not to take much river bank with it, as it ox-bowed it's way to the Missouri, down around Wolf Point some fifty miles away.

Dad revealed a can of worms he'd dug in the morning before I awoke. He had been planning this as a surprise. Spearing the earthworms on the hook the best I could and unwinding some of the line on the pole, I swung the line, hook/bait, sinker, cork, upstream as far as the line would allow. Ted was busy with his own equipment a little downstream from me. Dad was involved with his, just to my left, upstream. The idea was to watch the cork. As it inched its way downstream, if it started to pop down and up that meant a fish was biting on the worm on the hook. The trick was to wait till the bobber went all the way under and started to move upstream, then jerk the pole up, setting the hook,

and just pull the fish out of the water, over your head
onto dry land and jump on it, keeping it from flopping
back into the stream.

My cast left me mid-creek about 15 feet above
my position. The cork bobber was jerking those
annoying, but interesting, little bobs that meant minnows
were playing with the bait. When my line got about even
with me in its downstream course, the bobber went
totally under the surface of the water. It did not reappear.
My line started migrating upstream at a rapid pace.

"Set the hook, McGee!" Dad yelled.

"Whoa. What cha got there?" from Ted.

I didn't just set the hook. I was ready to pull this
giant out of the stream for good. As I pulled with all the
strength I could muster, a huge yellow carp gradually
appeared at the end of my line. He was so big that I
could almost count his scales. He rolled over and headed
for the bottom.

"Pull him on out," Dad was jumping towards me.

I pulled on the pole and Mr. Big Yellow Fish
came up towards the surface. Now he was completely
out of the water, airborne, and coming toward me and the
bank. At that exact moment Mr. Yellow spit out the
hook. Even though the momentum had him directed

towards the shore, he landed about a foot and a half short.

To my total surprise, Dad suddenly appeared knee deep in the water in front of me. "Come on you slippery bugger." He was reaching his hands all the way to the riverbed and in one fast, sweeping movement after another, scooping water and anything else that happened to get in his way, all over Ted and me. Suddenly he stopped and looking easily as amazed as Ted and I did began laughing. Soon all three of us caught the contagion and were roaring. I had never before felt that close to my dad.

We never did see anything more of Mr. Carp. I like to think he made it down to the *Mighty Mo* and beyond. Wherever he wound up, the experience made a fisherman of me for the rest of my life. What could be better? My Dad, whom I unconsciously emulated for the rest of my life, and me sharing this crazy bonding experience in a grand moment of kinship.

And that is why I fish!

SCOBEY: THE DUMPS AND THE DIPS

I suppose that every town has it's dumps. Scobey's was located Southeast of town about a mile or two away from inhabited ground. To this day I have to admit that I never knew who picked up the garbage in our alley. For a long time I had no idea where it was taken or what became of it. I suppose that one day I said something like, "Where is that smell coming from?" Or, pointing to the cloud of blue-ish/white-ish smoke rising in the distance, "What is that burning over there?"

Mom would have said, "Oh, that's just the dumps."

"The dumps? What're the dumps?"

"Well, Larry," she would have said, "You know how every now and again the garbage cans get emptied? Where do you suppose the garbage guys take it?"

"Interesting!"

We all had bikes by this time. My bike was a Gambles Hardware Special with shock absorbers on the front wheel. My bike tires were fat and tall. I had to start out with one leg dangled over the crossbar while I hopped one footed to get a start, jumping up on the seat just hoping I didn't get high centered on the crossbar. My next door neighbor, Alden, had what I thought was an alien bike. It had skinny tires that were also tall-that tire didn't look like a tire at all, and he had three speeds from which to choose. Uphill he would go down into a lower gear and petal twice as much but keep going. Sometimes I had to stop and walk my bike up to the top of the hill and then jump back on for an exciting ride down the other side.

We really enjoyed navigating new terrain on our bikes. We had walked most of the roads pulling my Radio Flyer wagon loaded with lunch or some other good thing but it was a new experience to do it by bike. We started out at our place and headed East. After about four blocks we began to run out of street. There was a barbed wire fence and on the other side was Rudy Nyquist's wheat field. More than once we had managed to get over, under or through the fence and taken the wagon, loaded with camping gear, up to the "S" Hill for an overnight camp-out. This time we decided to turn right (South) and follow that road for a while. As the buildings and streets began to recede into the distance we noticed the rows and rows of garbage two stories tall. Smoke was curling up out of some spots where an erstwhile garbage guy had ignited some piece of flotsam. Shoot! It might burn for a year once it got started.

We dismounted from our faithful steeds and decided to look around a bit. "Hey, Alden, if we find something here we want, we can just take it, right?"

"Yeah, I think so. Who's gonna tell us no?"

"You mean all these rows and rows and rows of stuff and it's all FREE?"

"Yeah, I do think so."

"WOW!!! FREE!!! FREE STUFF!!! WOW!!!"

We spent the rest of our time that day digging through discarded dreams and distant memories of people unknown. "Hey, look at this gizmo! What do you think it is?"

"That's a part of a electric motor or something."

"You know what, I've been reading about making a telegraph set. I'll bet the wire in this is copper. It sure looks like copper, don't you think?"

"Yeah, it sure does. Did you say a telegraph set?"

"Yeah, I got the plans for it on a cereal box. I cut it out and have been saving it for when I could get some wire. I'll show you when we get home."

"Okay."

"This stuff is sure dirty. I think they tried to burn it and it just didn't go up."

"WHOA!!! Did you see that?"

"What?"

"I think it was a giant rat. It went under that old car body over there."

I said, "Well, for me...I'm about ready to take my wire and go home. What do you say?"

"Yeah, you betcha."

THE TELEGRAPH SET

The wire was difficult to extract from the machine part I had discovered. It was copper wire coated with some sort of plastic insulating material. It was yards and yards long. Out came the directions I had saved from that cereal box. I sawed two pieces of one inch board, both about six inches by three inches. Pounding a spike into one of the boards until the point was coming out of the bottom, I wound the wire around the spike until it was a coil, an inch and a half wide along the entire spike. With my dad's tin snips I next tackled a Maxwell House coffee can making two, two inch wide strips three inches long and one two inch strip six inches long. Nailing the long strip of tin to the board with the coiled spike I formed a kind of arm hovering over the top of the spike.

Connecting to the positive terminal of a large dry cell phone battery and the other to the negative, an electric current was sent through the coil on the spike, creating a magnet that pulled the tin arm down causing a miniature click. Using the other piece of wood and the two strips of tin I fashioned a crude telegraph key, completing the set.

After another wire trip to the Rat Dump we had enough to create a set for Alden and Clive. On the next trip to the Rat Dump we found blasting wire from seismograph testing that could run from my house to the French house so we could telegraph each other. The fact that we didn't know the Morse Code didn't matter to us. The sets weren't reliable enough to differentiate between a dit and a daw anyway. We just enjoyed waking each other up in the morning. "The first one up gets to telegraph the other that he needs to wake up and get moving."

THE DIPS

We spent many enjoyable days at our FREE STUFF place. Digging in the dirty junk was delightful. Every once in a while we would see the _Giant Rat of the Dump._ We made a pact that we would come back with .22 Rifles and shoot him. In the meantime we decided we would like to examine the road that went beyond the dump. The road turned into more or less of a two rut pathway out over the hills. Alden's bike, with the three speed transmission was a little better suited to the climbing of hills than mine. Mine with the fat tires negotiated the rutted road a little better than his. It was a lot of fun to get to the top of a hill and then accelerate down the back side never using a brake because we wanted to see how far up we could get on the next hill. It was a series of hills and valleys that stretched a couple miles until it met up with the highway further West that ran from Scobey to Wolf Point.

We enjoyed it enough to put together a contingent of Bikers numbering five or six. I don't remember exactly who was in the group when we had the largest posse on wheels, but I would venture a compliment consisting of Alden and Clive French, John Brenden, David Solberg and myself. We were out near the middle of the dips when we decided to turn back. It may have been a little more than a couple of miles from our homes. There were a daring duo out front, leading the way, followed by David, then me, then maybe John. We had just struggled up one of the uphill segments and were starting down with the wind in our hair and eyes. Suddenly, David, on the bike in front of me lost control of his front wheel in a rut. The bike jack knifed back over front throwing David on the ground face first. I brought my bike to a stop and yelled for everyone to stop. Jumping from my bike I got to David just in time to see him start to come to. He had honestly landed on his face in the gravel ruts. His face was starting to bleed from a series of cuts where gravel had embedded itself in his forehead and chin and cheeks and arms. Everyone was now standing around looking at the mess and not knowing what to do. To add to the confusion as brave as he had been, David began to cry. I said, "I'll try to get some of the gravel out of your face, David."

As I reached down to pick a rather large stone out of his flesh he cried out, "Don't touch it. I got to get home right away!" With that we righted his bike which was in riding condition and he got on and we started for town. Every time I think of that accident, I am amazed at David's bravery and fearlessness.

I was listening to a book the other day that brought this occasion to mind. I'm trying to remember the author's name...No luck...Here is what he said:

BECAUSE WE WEREN'T HOVERED OVER EVERY SECOND OF OUR LIVES WE LEARNED HOW TO FALL

Here's to all the Davids of the world!

The .22 Caliber Luger Pistol

Growing up in the West in the 40's and 50's a person might assume that one would grow up with respect and even a bit of an awe of armament. That was the case for a large number of families. Others took more or less the approach that the children had average intelligence and therefore would not have to be taught how to handle rifles and pistols. What could there possibly be about a gun that would be difficult to understand? I mean, revolving cylinders that hold a ready supply of unused shells, or magazines, tubular or internal, that serve the same purpose are intuitively constructed so that all a person has to do is look at them and *voila*! You understand.

The cleaning and caring for fire arms may be a different matter. Some folks took their youth on a marathon of cleaning and proper storage instruction. Others, just assumed that as long as the rifle or pistol sat unused it should be ready to go at a moments notice. I believe that my dad was of the sort that assumed his children would be intelligent enough to take sufficient care of what ever fire arms they came across. His idea of proper gun training was, "Never assume a gun is empty, always treat a gun as if it were loaded, and NEVER, NEVER, NEVER POINT A GUN AT ANYTHING THAT YOU DIDN'T WANT TO SHOOT!"

My first love with a rifle was the .22 Caliber Remington Pump that was kept in a corner of the utility room out of sight and out of mind. (Not out of my mind) It had an octagonal barrel, a tubular magazine capable of holding well over ten .22 short cartridges, an exposed hammer that the opening block cocked automatically when you "pumped" a new shell into the firing chamber. I handled that rifle like it was gold. Back in the utility room with the door shut, I could pump that action and dry fire it without interruption from mom or my little sister, Joanne or my big brother Donald. I can't tell you how many dead wild Indians cluttered the utility room or the outside area where I could shoot them through the windows with impunity. The bodies just piled up and up and up. Placing the rifle back in it's obscurity, I would calmly saunter out the utility room door and answer mom's query, "Whatchya been up to Larry?" with, "Oh, nothing much. Just got a bunch of those Indians that have been bothering us so much."

Mom's answer would have been, "Oh, that's nice. Why don't you run along and play outside for a while?"

Not too much later, I discovered a full box of .22 Shorts tucked away in a drawer that had no idea the treasure it held. Good old Utility Room!!! Now I can load the rifle with real bullets. No stopping me now. Birds and gophers beware. Sharp shooter on the loose. Putting the box of bullets in my pocket and taking the gun out of obscurity, I proceeded to the door. I marched right out into the kitchen and through the living/dining room, into the entry way and out into the front yard. "Hey, Larry! What in the world are you doing with that gun?"

"I'm just going hunting," I replied.

"Larry, you're too young to go hunting. You need to talk with your dad all about it first, you know."

Very grown up about it all, "That's okay, Mom. Dad and I had a long talk about it all and I can tell you everything he told me. <u>Always treat a gun like it's loaded, Never think a gun is empty, and Don't point at anything you don't want to shoot.</u>"

Mom shook her head and said, "He never told me anything about any of this."

"It's okay, Mom! All those Indians I shot were just pretend. I'm not going to shoot anything but old gophers."

It's kind of hard to believe, but she let me go out to the East edge of town which was about three of four blocks away. I did go out and shoot a few fence posts and a couple of rocks. I loved the sound they made when the bullet zinged off of them and went God knows where.

That's the way I was taught gun safety!!!

FAST FORWARD TO HIGH SCHOOL

The school year was 1956/57. When dad built the addition onto the house in 1955 (?) he built a second floor which housed my room and my brother Don's room and a big closet for annual stuff. When Don left home upon graduation from High School, I got to move into his room. It was a little bigger than my room and had closets on the side of the wall where the roof slopped upward. The two closets both had plywood doors and home made door frames that were about four feet tall.

Every now and then I would examine the closets to see if I had missed anything the last time I had scavenged them. At one point I put my fingers of both hands onto the top of the door frame and to my surprise I felt something there I hadn't discovered before. I drew down a .22 Caliber pistol. My brother must have hidden it there before leaving home and just left it. It was a semi-automatic Luger lookalike. Wow!!! After looking it over a little I decided it could be my secret weapon. I had learned from dad not to dry fire guns because it could damage the firing pin. I just replaced it in it's hiding place of three years. If it could stay undiscovered for as long as it had, it could remain for another many years.

One of my good friends, John Brenden and I ate lunch away from the school. We both walked home at noon from school, me to my home and John to his grandmother's house that was kind of kitty corner from my house. We formed a habit of John finishing his lunch and then stopping for me at my place for the return to school two blocks further. We started playing the card game "WAR" up in my room to while away a few minutes before retracing our steps to school.

One day while up in my room I said, "John. Can you keep a secret?"

John replied, "Sure. Whatchya got?"

I simply walked over to the closet, opened the door, reached up and pulled out what looked like a German Luger. John's response was, "Wow! What a cool gun. Who's is it?"

I said, "Well, I guess it must be mine. I'm sure my brother Don put it up there, but he's gone so…"

At that point, in my best Jimmy Cagney imitation, I poked the gun right into John's belly and said, "Don't move a muscle, ya dirty rat!"

John brushed the gun away and said, "I don't like having guns pointed at me!"

To which I replied, "Oh, it isn't loaded. Watch!" I then pointed the gun at the floor and pulled the trigger. That was the loudest BANG I had ever heard. With eyes open wide and hands shaking and heart doing a Clydesdale gallop, I was unable to form any words. It was then that mom called upstairs, "What was that big bang?"

I lied, "Oh, we just found an old fire cracker and it worked."

"Oh, well, isn't it time for you two to be getting back to school?"

"Yah, we're on the way."

Why do I believe in Hunter Safety?

Summer Fallow

Sitting here at my computer, thinking about doing the summer fallowing, I'm frankly stuck on how to get started. I think I should start out by giving a brief description of that dry land farm. This entire area of Montana had been under a glacier during the last Ice Age. Residual boulders were distributed over thousands of years that ice ruled the land. The soil was not very deep and there were a lot of gravel deposits near the surface. Through the "Dirty Thirties" (the 1930's had been a decade of drought and wind) part of the top soil had been blown into Nebraska and parts East. A large part of Montana and Wyoming is lying under deceptive grass covered dunes called the Sand Hills of Northern Nebraska.

Following those years, the farmers began to practice strip farming and summer fallowing. A strip of land as long as was practical and about eighty feet across (my guess-ta-met) would be laid out and sown to the prevalent crop. Usually Hard Red Spring Wheat, or Winter Wheat or Barley was the choice. Then next to that strip would be another same shaped piece of land that was allowed to lie fallow for the growing season. And so the practice of alternating the strips was followed by most all the farmers. The problem was that the fallow land grew weeds like crazy. Here I have to interrupt this narrative with one of my favorite jokes as follows:

The farmer was at work in his beautiful field and the preacher drove by. Seeing the farmer at work he stopped to compliment him on his bountiful crop. "The Lord has certainly blessed you with a beautiful and bountiful field, hasn't he?" the preacher asked. To which the farmer replied, "Yes sir, he certainly has. But you ought to have seen it when he had it all to himself." (Heh-heh)

So before the weeds could take over, they had to be knocked down. Dad's choice of implement for doing so was what was called a tool bar. Back in the day the tool bar was twelve feet wide. With three or four rows of "Duck Foot" shovels, on the end of spring loaded supports that hanged down from the frame, they scraped under the ground at a depth of about six to ten inches disturbing the roots of the weeds enough to interrupt their growth while the merciless July/August sun dried them out.

Our tractor was a McCormick-Deering WD-9. It ran on Diesel fuel. It had a gas starter engine that you had to start first when you were getting going. 1. Start up the starter engine and let it warm up. 2. Make sure your transmission was in neutral. 3. Start the main engine and give it a little fuel. 4. Everything should be ready to go.

Dad was a believer in doing everything as correctly as possible. He knew that if you ran the tractor in too high a gear, the tool bar would not disturb the weeds roots enough to stunt their growth. Since that was the reason we were "Summer Fallowing" he insisted that I remain in second gear as I guided the equipment up and down the mile and a half long strips. To a teenager, that was like an inch a minute. Oh Lord, those strips were long. I couldn't think of where I would have been or what I might have been doing if I had been able to go a little faster. All I could do was sit sideways on the tractor seat, (you had to be able to keep one eye on the tool bar behind you and one eye on where you were going) and ride that baby into oblivion.

In the early morning, when it was still fairly cool, it was almost enjoyable. I was King of the tractor people, saving the land from the blight of weeds. I was careful to be sure of the depth of the shovels. Rows straight as a die. Dad was extremely particular about straight rows. As we passed other farmers fields it was, "Oh, my God!!! Look at those crooked rows!!!" or "Say now, Old Clyde seems to know what he's doing. Check those straight rows." He would say, "Now McGee, just pick out a feature of any kind on the horizon and aim toward that. That's the secret to a straight row." And I'd be on my way. (Or "**on my weigh**" depending whether on land or sea)

You know, that summer fallowing was one of the **dirt**iest jobs in the world. There always seemed to be a following breeze out on the strip. When you got to the end of the strip and turned the equipment to make a return pass on the other side of the strip, the wind shifted like it was controlled by some demon. You found yourself in a constant cloud of dust which followed you everywhere. You just got covered with dust about an eighth of and inch thick.

Around noon dad would show up and "spell" me for a round while I ate lunch. Mom always packed great lunches. Special sandwiches that I thought were great, cool milk, a Tootsie Roll so I could make my version of chocolate milk right in my mouth, and a hard boiled egg. In the venue of a clean kitchen with hands that have been washed and the absence of dirt in general, it is a pretty simple matter to peel a hard boiled egg. Boy, oh boy! Out in the dirty world peeling an egg is….Well suffice it to say that I would look at that egg that had been peeled by my hands and say to myself, "My, my, my, my, my! Am I going to eat that dirty thing?" And of course, Down it went. A little salt and pepper and it was gone. I'm fairly sure that who ever said that you have to eat your peck of dirt, didn't mean all at once!

And HOT!!! I'm sure that when the sun passed it's zenith and it got to be around 1:30-3:30 PM that the temperature zoomed up to at least ninety degrees. Sitting out on the tractor without any umbrella, the heat from the engine being fanned right at you, the dust choking you, the endless rattle and clatter of the equipment, a person could go crazy. I carried a gallon bottle wrapped in a gunny sack, tied with twine, full of water. It had been nice and cool when I filled it out of the hose in the early morning, but now… at least it was wet.

In the mind numbing heat, dust, and noise my mind would begin to pick up the repetitious sounds coming from the equipment. Rat-a-tat-tat-tat from the little exhaust cover. Skree-onch skree skree from metal on metal. The huge tires growling the protest of rubber on gravel. Suddenly, an entire orchestra had formed in my mind. High strings and woodwinds doing scales in triplets Tra-la-la, Tra-la-la, Tra-la-la Laa. Trombones simultaneously on scales down to the bottom Du-du-du, Du-du-du, Du-du-du, Duu. Trumpets and Saxophones thundering three part chords, Cymbals clanging, Bass Drum Booming, Snare Drums snaring away. Standing up and directing, one hand on the wheel, one hand cuing this section, that section. Toes tapping the meter. And I hear a very faint sound of a voice in the midst of the grand cacophony. Looking behind me, who is running to catch the run-away equipment? It was DAD!!! It is then that I realize I'm out in the middle of the strip. Oh God! No straight row award today!

Dad, laying on his back, trying to catch his asthmatic breath gasped, "You damn near killed me, McGee, running like that! You could've killed yourself! What in the HELL were you thinking?"

Being totally unable to fashion any kind of sensible reason for my actions I fell back on my good old excuse, "By golly,"--(pause, shaking my head left then right, then up and down, left then right)--, "I JUST DON'T KNOW!"

MY FRIEND RUSSELL (WENDY) NEW AND ME

Growing up in Scobey, Montana in the 1940's and 50's was much like a larval unit maturing in a cocoon. The great world outside of our town was so foreign it might as well have been Outer Mongolia. We received letters from it on occasion, notifications of relatives deaths by the two-party telephone, and news reel shorts at the movies, but the only other contact we had with it was through the radio. My folks, Francis and Beulah Brasen, thought enough about the world beyond the 14 mile trip to the farm, that they bought a radio for the family. I believe that Joanne and Bernie Gilbert still have that same radio. It was a magnificent piece of furniture as well as "THE" entertainment center for everyone in the house. Quite honestly I believe it was here that I learned to listen. It is a skill I've honed for the rest of my life, and it has done me many wonderful favors. Critical listening and remembering is an essential skill not only in music in general, but also in learning and evaluating people and concepts. As a Freshman in High School, I was more aware of a world around us because of the winters Joanne and I spent with our folks in Arizona in 1952-53 and 1953-54. Those experiences also made me more alert to differences in people, in their actions and reactions to people and situations.

Viewing my world through the eyes of a partially awakened Larval Peeper, I noticed that a boy named Wendy New had a different way about him. One thing I noticed right away in class was that he had difficulty pronouncing words that started with the letter P. I suppose you might call it stuttering except that it mainly only happened on "P" words. Some of the guys and gals in the class snickered under their breath when it happened. (Under their breath but loud enough for Wendy to hear them.) I thought to myself, how smart does a guy need to be to construct entire paragraphs in his head before answering a question to make sure there would be no "P" words in the answer? He didn't speak up much in class but I thought it was because of his difficulty speaking. I got to know Wendy through the program that was called The Early Advance Warning System. (I made up the name but it was something like that.)

The EAWS was a system put into affect by the National Government to give advance warning of planes crossing into the United States from Canada. The whole idea was to have someone watching the skies and listening for the airplane engines twenty four hours a day. Our town chose the site on top of the Fire House. They built a little shack on the flat roof of the Fire Department, provided it with windows to the North, South, East and West. The windows could be slid horizontally so they could be opened for better sighting and sound. They provided us with a book of outlines of enemy planes so the person on guard could "identify" the culprit and then report it by telephone direct to the nearest Air Force Base out of Great Falls, Montana so they could scramble an intercept force. This was someones idea of the best defense system we could mount. These observation posts were strung along the entire Canadian border from East to West. As Freshmen in High School, Wendy and I were signed up for service and we took our tours of duty together. As time wore on people just quit taking their service as seriously as they had in the beginning. The log book went many times unsigned by members of the <u>Ground Observers Corps</u>. (There, I remembered what it was called.) This fact opened an opportunity that Wendy and I could take advantage of. We really wanted to get our One Hundred Hour Badges to put on our jackets Soooo….

You guessed it!!! We decided to pull an all nighter. We already had a lot of hours built up from just regular shifts and we figured it out that if we pulled an extra sixteen hours we would qualify for the badges. Of course we couldn't tell our parents what we were contemplating so we sat down with a cup of coffee at the Cozy Cafe just down from Forchacks Pool Hall. (When I say coffee I mean a little coffee and a lot of sugar. I couldn't stand the taste of straight coffee.) Sooo…

The Plot Thickens

"You tell your folks that I invited you to stay over with me. I'll tell my folks you invited me to stay over with you. We'll meet at the GOC shack on top of the Fire Hall."

Wendy, "If we're going to stay up all night, we'll need to get some stuff to eat and drink. I can bring a coffee pot. Can you get some coffee?"

Me, "Sure. How about some chocolate chip cookies? I can dig some out of our freezer."

Wendy, "Great! We should have something for sandwiches. Bread and peanut butter?"

Me, "Okay. I can get like half a loaf of bread, can you get the peanut butter?"

And sooo… the story goes.

It was early Fall and the sun was still shining into the early evening when we met at the appointed place and time. I had stowed all my stuff in a Boy Scout backpack and lugged it down to the shack. Wendy showed up with all his stuff and we set up an inventory of all the goodies we had. A couple extra bottles of Pepsi... I remember breakfast muffins...Coffee and a pot and cups furnished by the GOC.

About that time, we heard the drone of a far off AIRCRAFT!!! Holy Crap!!! What now? Wendy said, "Can you see where it is? What kind of Plane is it?"

"I can't see anything. It's starting to get dark. It sounds like it's up North", I said.

Wendy said, "We need to report it to the Air Force in Great Falls!" And with that I picked up the Red Phone and looked at the suddenly very heavy object in my hand. I managed to get the receiver to my ear in time to hear a male voice intoning, "Malstrom here! Your report!"

Try as I might, nada, nothing, nil, zip, zero was coming out of my mouth. Not realizing that I hadn't breathed in a while, all I could do was stand there with mouth agape, looking at the phone in hand, and pointing to it with my left hand.

Wendy took the phone, and started a report that went something like, "We saw, heard a Paa." It was here that the dreaded "P" word came up. Wendy's cheeks puffed out and his lips were sealed totally shut. Wordlessly he handed me back the phone.

I said, "A plane. We heard a plane. It was North of us. We couldn't see it. And then it was gone."

"Just where are you gentlemen located?"

That was it! I hung up the phone. If Russia bombed us this night, no one was going to blame Wendy and me.

"Pass me a chocolate chip cookie, Wendy."

"Yeah, Okay!"

The View From The Top

Scobey is out on the Northeastern Plains of Montana. Not many trees unless you count the cottonwoods living along the few streams meandering on their way down to the Mighty Mo down around the town of Wolf Point. No mountains majesty rising from the plain to touch the sky or the clouds or to frame the boundaries of your existence. Many times as a teen, riding to the farm several miles Northwest of town, Dad and I would share the incredible sight of a mirage in the sky due West of us. Dad tried to explain the phenomenon as two air masses of different density creating a kind of mirror that looked down on the mountains and refracted the image into the sky. We thought the mountains we were seeing were the Little Rocky Mountains out of Havre.

The tallest thing in the area was the water tower looming over a hundred feet in the air. It held the water necessary for maintaining life in the community whether it be for drinking, bathing, lawns, gardens, car washes (We didn't know about keeping your car glistening like new all year long), or splashing each other with water balloons. When driving to Scobey from Wolf Point, the game in the car was, "Who can see the water tower first?" It was never where we thought it was going to be. As kids growing up the tower was always just that. It was the Tower! We thought it had always probably been there and would always continue to be there, standing guard over the community it protected and provided the wonderful life stuff called water.

Did you ever notice how the water of every community tasted different. Each seemed to have it's own taste. You would not notice it if you never went out of the town where you were born. But as soon as I went to Plentywood and drank a glass of water there, I was amazed how different it tasted. Wolf Point in the cafe was I can't begin to tell you. UGH!!! I'm sure that the different tastes in towns was due to mineral content in the water. Our water was from wells, God knows where, and then pumped into town and up to the top of the tower. Once you got accustomed to the taste it seemed just natural and quite refreshing.

What is it about human beings that they are totally unable to leave well enough alone? When I reached a certain age, the water tower took on an entirely new and interesting persona. It was as though it personally was engaging me with a challenge. It's very existence was an affront to me. It had to be investigated, understood, a plan made and conquered. I started with a reconnoitering mission. Up the block and a half to the site of the tower. Walk around the property eyeing the weaknesses of the surrounding hedge and fence. Once on the South side of the tower estate, I discovered a gate. Safer from prying eyes, I worked the gate until with my slender frame I could slip through into the actual tower domain. Finally inside the guardian hedge, I was able to recon out of the sight of neighbors and busy bodies. Wow! What a huge, beautiful tower. I felt it was my own possession. The rest of the world was totally shut out. It was just the tower and me.

She had four legs. Each leg was a foot wide I-beam with thick steel strap exes across the back and the front. Strongly made! "This is good!" On the Northwest leg starting at ten feet, was a ladder right up the outside of the leg and at the base of the tank the ladder straightened up and climbed right up to the catwalk all the way around the tower. What a view that would be!!! I next turned my attention to the rectangular housing built to enclose the pipes that carry water up to the tank and back down to supply the town with water.

I discovered a door into the housing. Trying the door I found it locked. There was no hasp and lock on the door. There was no metal plate with a keyhole in it. "I'll be darned! This baby is locked from the inside!" It must be a hook and eye latch. That means there has to be access to the inside from up on top of the housing. Okay, I guess the thing to do would be to climb up the inside of the leg with the ladder, get even with the ladder and swing around with one hand and one foot, clamber around, climb the ladder up to the top of the area at the bottom of the tank where there appeared to be a plank construction over to the top of the housing and examine that.

I found climbing on the exes on the back of the leg with the ladder to be relatively easy. I noted that the next time I did this, maybe I would profit from a pair of gloves. I got up to the level where the ladder was on the other side of the leg. I put my right foot out and onto the lowest rung. It was on the rung in a crooked way, but it was the best I could manage. I reached around with my right hand and found the rung at that level. I hadn't even glanced at the ground. Now I looked down and my heart about jumped out of my body. I was about twenty feet above the ground and that's enough to scare most sane people. My heart was pumping wildly in my ears. With eyes wide open I let go of my left hand hold and swung my body and hand and foot around and was standing on the first rung of the ladder. "Phew!" Well, let's get on up to the level with the planks at the very bottom of the tank.

There were two 2X12 planks side by side leading over to the top of the housing. They were painted a sort of gray which the water tower was painted at that time. They were suspended over what looked like a drop to the ground of about sixty to eighty feet by lag bolts on one end and a metal strap fashioned from 3/8 inch iron about two inches wide and attached to the ladder so they were somewhat stable. Looking over at the top of the housing which was now visible, I saw a hinged trap door. It was asking to be opened and probed to My satisfaction. There was nothing to do but to crawl over to the housing and open the door and see what was on the inside.

I put my left foot on the planks. Felt Okay...stomped on it a couple times...Pretty solid...Both feet...jumped up and down holding onto the ladder...I'm guessing it will hold my weight. Getting down on my hands and knees, I reached out with my right hand and grabbed the side of the plank. Doing the same with my left hand I was ready to crawl. Slowly I inched my way over the plank bridge. About the time I got half way I began to detect a little swaying in the planks. Now was the time to get going forward or just back up and give up. Forward Ho the wagons...before I knew it the roof of the housing was under my hands and knees. Reaching over with my right hand I tested the lid. It was loose enough to pry up. With little effort the lid lifted on it's hinges, swung up and over and kerplop...I was looking down into the interior of the housing. There was a ladder on the inside made of 2 X 4s nailed in the corner to the wall of the housing.

I was suddenly inside with the sound of dripping water, the mustiness of ages, the odor of water soaked wood covered with greenish mold, Dank longing for the sun, and Spider webs...Oh My God, Spiders!!! I did not, do not, and will not like spiders!!! Webs, webs and more webs. My eyes grew more accustomed to the dark and it looked like the main pipe coming down from the tower was actually another wooden casing. Looking down it was difficult to make out the bottom down at ground level. Making out the next step down (about two feet apart) I make my way down. One of the 2 X 4 rungs had been nailed in place another six inches further from the one I was standing on. Looking down it was possible to just make out the step just beyond my foot feeling around. Easing down on it, I made the rest of the way to the ground level. Never had so many cob webs on my face and arms. The only light in the place was from the trap door way up above there. It was a little square of light in a vast darkness. Tripping over flotsam of some sort the door to the outside was at hand. Squinting and fumbling...Hah!!! The latch!!! I knew it!!! It popped up and the door swung open allowing the fresh air and sunlight to pierce the gloom and dank of the housing. Alright!!! Finding a stray brick to prop the door shut my first Tower Adventure was complete!!!

STAY TUNED FOR PART 2 AND BEYOND

The View From The Top (Part 2)

Upon completion of my First Tower Adventure, I went on a Wheaties for breakfast campaign. WHEATIES; BREAKFAST OF CHAMPIONS!!! My buddy, Alden, my next door neighbor, and good friend, and I had shared a couple of experiences climbing the water tower Inside Out. So far we hadn't gone up to the catwalk that circumnavigated the entire tank. Our activities had been limited to the outside of the leg with the ladder and inside the housing. (We stashed a flashlight on the ground floor for further adventures.) To go the rest of the way up was going to require total loyalty to the "Breakfast of Champions" diet. While eating my breakfast one fine day, I noticed that in 1952 Bob Richards had stunned the world winning the Olympic Pole Vaulting Championship. Richards was quoted right on the package, **"When you throw your heart over the bar, your body has to follow."** <u>WOW!!!</u>

I had seen "Movie Time News Reels" at the Rex Theater that showed Bob achieving his historic vaults. We didn't have anything like that at the school in Scobey, so I decided that I would build a jumping bar in the back yard. When finished the structure looked a little like the football goal posts. It had two upright 2 X 4s stuck in the ground that had hand-drilled holes the size of match sticks (no electric drills), an eight foot dowel for a cross bar, match sticks stuck in the holes to hold the dowel. When it came to the pole we had a disassembled long handled shovel. Not too long but I thought it might be about right for starters.

So I grabbed the "pole", got back a little bit, ran right up to the jump with the pole in the air like Bob Richards did in the news reel, put the pole on the ground and just kind of stood there. There was something about that whole deal I obviously didn't understand. Putting the bar at the three foot level, I decided to just jump it. Didn't need the pole.

Giving Alden, the secret "Whippoorwill Whistle" three times, I waited to see if he would respond. We met at the hedge between our two gardens. Alden started the conversation with, "Hey! Whatcha up to?" To which I replied, "Just finished my jumping thing. Want ta give it a try?" Alden answered, "Not right now. I gotta finish weeding this row first. I saw you were doing something with lumber and stuff. Maybe when I get done with this row, I'll give it a go."

"Speaking of weeding, how are your carrots doing? Ours are still really small. I like the taste of 'em, but we need to let them grow up a little before we pull 'em and eat 'em."

Alden said, "Same with ours. Too small. I think we needed to plant 'em sooner."

"I wonder about Brownie's. They had theirs in way before we did." Selmer and Brownie Nelson lived across the alley from Pat and Muriel Horton and us. I believe they had three kids. I think there were two boys older than me and then Ann, our age,

"I don't know. How can we find out?", Alden asked.

"Why don't we ask Ann? She'd know. She's been weeding over there. I saw her."

"All right", we said together.

We both looked over in that direction, but no Ann was to be found.

"Well, later then."

"Hey, Alden, you wanna hit the tower after dark?"

"I don't know. Whatdcha have in mind?"

"How about maybe hitting the apple tree across from John's place? Those are getting really nice for eating. We could take them up and eat them up there."

"Okay, let's get together after supper."

Later that afternoon I was burning the garbage when Ann said, "Hi, Larry. Whatcha doing?"

"Not much. Just burning the garbage."

Ann said, "I saw you working on that thing you got in your yard. What are you doing there?"

"Oh, you mean my jumping place. I'm just trying to be like Bob Richards on the Wheaties box. You know, pole vaulting."

"How does that work?" Ann asked.

"Well, to tell you the truth, I haven't figured it out yet."

"Say, Ann, I noticed our carrots aren't big enough to eat yet. How are yours doing now?"

"Oh, I'll pull one for you."

She reached down in the garden and came up with a beautiful carrot nearly six inches long and one inch in diameter at the top. "Here, you can have it." She handed it to me.

"Wow, thanks," I said, making a mental note to be sure to tell Alden about the carrots there later. Did you ever notice how fresh and sweet carrots are right out of the garden? I mean, you can try to get all the dirt off of them but no matter what you do, some of it just goes in the mouth. And you don't even care. If you did the same thing inside your house you'd be spitting and lip wiping like crazy. But boy oh boy, when you're in the garden, all the other rules just don't apply.

After supper that evening, Alden and Clive and I went up to Solberg's front yard where we gathered often to play "Kick the Can" and "Red Rover, Red Rover, send (*insert name*) right over". We also would play a version of Kick the can with high power flash lights. The person that was "It" had the light and when he was able to flash the light on one of the players he had to call out "One, Two, Three on David", at which time David had to come in to the center area and surrender himself. At the appropriate time the Solberg parents called a halt to the games and we all dispersed to our homes. Well, not All.

Alden and I separated from the other kids and walked on the other side of the street in the general direction of Home. When we came to the street light, we took a left turn and then a right turn down the alley and we were found ourselves precisely at the garden of Selmer and Brownie Nelson. It was dark in the alley. It was exactly the condition we had anticipated. The Nelson's garbage cans were perfect to hide behind to make our last minute plan of action.

"Okay. I know where the carrots are growing, so you follow me into the garden. No hogging of the carrots. Take two at most. We don't want to leave any evidence that anyone has been in the garden. Now, if anybody comes out and thinks they see something, I'll hide behind the corn right over there and you get back behind the garbage cans. Okay?"

"Okay!"

We came out from behind the 55 gallon garbage cans on all fours. Nobody made a sound. I got to the row where the carrots were and put my hand of a piece of glass cutting into the palm of my hand. "Ouch", I said.

Alden said, "What happened?"

"Something sharp on my hand," I grimaced.

We had just picked a couple of carrots when the lights went on in the garage and someone with a deep voice said, "Is anybody there?"

Whispering, "Plan 2."

Alden said, "Huh?"

"Get down!"

We were down for the count by the time a big man (supposedly Selmer Nelson) came around the corner with a flash light. "I have a shotgun here. If anybody's here, you better come out right now."

A gun!!! A Shotgun!!! I felt my eyes bugging out of my head. For God's sake, Alden. Don't Breathe. I didn't need to remind myself, Don't even Breathe. You ever notice how time slows way down sometimes and then speeds back up double time to make up for the lapse? Those ten or fifteen seconds where we were in the garden in the corn and behind the cans lasted forever. Then he turned on his heel and went back into the garage. I don't remember exactly when I began breathing again. I just have to assume I did. Sneaking down to the end of the garden at the alley, I sort of crawled over the little fence guarding the garden. Alden was right behind the Horton's garbage cans on the other side of the alley. Alright! Now, up the alley to the apple tree.

The street lights were on the corners of intersecting streets. It was dark in the alley and across the road to the Brenden's garage. From here the apple tree was only a few steps across the alley and there we were. When you've been in the dark for a while, you begin to notice you can see more than you thought you could. The apples were kind of shining in the moonlight. It was as though they were just asking to be picked and eaten. "Now remember, we're only taking what we can eat. No waste."

Pockets full, we finish our trip up the alley past The Teigen's, The Trower's and past the last house before the street. There in the moonlight gleamed our beautiful Tower. We were just able to make out the protective hedge and fence surrounding it with the light available. We walked all the way around it on the West side away from the street light on the corner. Now on the South side we made our way to the gate. Slipping through, we found ourselves once again in the relative security of the inner sanctum. Guarded on all sides by the hedge we were temporarily invisible for all practical purposes. Time for a strategy session.

"You know what," I started, "We have never been up to the catwalk. It's dark enough tonight to go up the ladder leg, and when we get to the planks over to the housing, we just go right on up and over onto the catwalk. What do you think?"

"Well, you know how the ladder goes straight up from the housing instead of kind of sloping on the leg? You thinking you're up for that?"

"We never did it before because it was in the daylight. Here's the deal. Since it's dark out, we can't see the ground to get scared, Right? If you want to I'll go first. No fair eating any more of the carrots or apples until we get on the catwalk, Okay?"

"All right. If you're up to it, so am I," Alden rejoined.

Once again we started up the inside of the leg with the ladder. I led the way and Alden was right behind me. This was always the tricky part, where you had to change from the inside "exes" to the ladder. Once on the rungs of the ladder, I felt secure. I glanced down in time to see Alden make the switch over from the "exes" to the ladder. Now at the part where the ladder changed its angle of ascent to true perpendicular, I felt a sharp intake of breath. As I climbed, I looked back down. Apparently I had lied when I said it was dark enough that we wouldn't get scared when we looked down. With Alden right behind me, I couldn't back down. I had to go up and go up I did. When I got to the catwalk I hastily scuttled over the three foot fence and looked down for Alden. His head popped up over the fence as I looked for him.

"You need any help coming over the fence?" I asked.

"No thanks." Alden crawled over the fence structure and was safe on the catwalk with me.

"Hey, Alden, You shaking?"

"Naw, not too bad."

"Yeah, me neither."

"Well, let's sit down and have a bite to eat."

"Doggone, just look at the town from here. You can see Main Street all lit up. And there's the school."

"Yeah, and there's your place and mine. And there's the ghost house. And look over there, the hospital."

"Wow, this is really great."

There is something undefinable about the joy of eating stolen food after an illegal climb that scares you spitless but you feel safe in the dark. Just take the time to truly experience the joy of achievement and don't even think about the time you'll have to return to the world of risk.

And there is something to be said for being of an age where most of life's lessons still lie in front of you. When you are on top of the world...what could possibly happen. There was nothing anyone could have said that would have convinced me that I wasn't invincible.

STAY TUNED FOR THE TOWER TRILOGY: THE
FINALE

The View From The Top: Finale

This beautiful Fall day started with the clickity/clangidy sound of our home made tin telegraph asking to be answered. I hopped out of bed and over to my desk where the set was presently residing. Closing the key which should have shut it off as a signal that I would respond, it continued it's ratchity clicking. Thinking about the circuitry I decided to unhook the thing from the battery. That did that! There is nothing as wonderful as a Saturday morning after school has started in the Autumn. I had planned out what I was going to do today.

Number one, I had to break the fast of the eventide with Bob Richards and his Wheaties. After some household chores, I planned on using a new method of high jumping on my back yard cross bar. It was called the Scissor Jump. I had heard of it from one of the teachers at school. You run at the bar from your right side and when you get to the bar you lift your right leg up as high as you can while you jump with your left leg. As you go over the bar with your butt, you lift your left leg as high as you can, making the action of a scissor. After practicing that for a while, I would whistle up Alden and see what he might want to do.

One thing for sure, we had to check our wire for the telegraph sets. The only thing I could think of was

there must be a short somewhere along the route. That
would probably mean taking the wire down all the way.
Kind of hate to do that after getting it up there like that.
Maybe it would be for the best. My Dad had said
something about it not being safe in case of lightning. I
had started to get tired of it anyway. You really couldn't
make any sense of the clicks and clacks as far as the
Morse code was concerned. I tackled the bowl of
Wheaties, milk, and sugar with with a big tablespoon.
Breakfast was important for the start of the day, but it
didn't have to take forever. All during the spooning and
crunching and finally the smunching (the last of the
Wheaties were always mushy) I concentrated on the
vision of me going over the bar and kicking with my left
leg, doing the scissor kick. As I went outside to weed the
potatoes, I thought about the kick. (When I say "Weed
the Potatoes" I really mean pick the bugs off the plants
and put them in a glass jar of water.) Finally, it's time to
practice the Scissor Kick Jump!

I had been going over it in my mind every step of
the way with the exception of the landing. It just never
occurred to me that could be a problem. The teacher that
told me about the jump hadn't mentioned anything about
the landing. If you got over the bar what could possibly
go wrong? With this in mind, you might guess that there
was about to be one of life's learning opportunities
happening. I got back away from the bar. I started out
slow with big steps. I gained speed. I got to the bar and

stopped dead in my tracks. The bar was set at three feet. Just a practice run. I did it again and this time up I went. As I flew over the bar with my right leg and then kicked my left leg over, my head hit the ground before anything else could happen. First my head, then my elbows, then my rear end and finally my feet. It was just solid ground.

Waking up, I wondered what happened. Then the pain. My head, my arms, my back, my legs, my feet and my everything else… Yeowch!!! I just laid there and that was when I heard our "Triple Whippoorwill Call". I looked over at the French's yard and saw Alden standing at the hedge.

"Wow! You really jumped it", from Alden.

Looking up at the bar still in place I replied, "Yeah, I guess I did. Hey, Alden! What do you say we hit the water tower today? We could slip up there this morning and I been thinking about going all the way to the top."

Alden didn't reply right away. Then he said, "Yeah. All the way to the top you think?"

"Well, we could just go up there to the tower, climb a little and see what happens after that."

"Yeah. I guess so. You think right now?"

"Sure. Let's go!" I suggested.

On our way up to the water tower we passed some of our friends that lived on the way. They asked, "You guys gonna climb the tower?"

To which we replied, "Maybe. Wait and see."

After arriving at the tower and accessing our way through the gate we had a moment for planning our assault. "Let's go up the inside of the housing so we don't attract too much attention on our way up. Once we come out of the trap door up there, we can decide what we want to do then. Okay?"

Inside the housing at the bottom we decided to just leave the door ajar. The trap door on the top was open so there was a little light inside. We had a flashlight that we had stashed earlier but when we tried turning it on the battery had about died all the way. It was too dim to use and besides, if we climb up on the 2 X 4 ladder we would need both hands free. So we began the climb up to the top of the housing. One nice thing was that there were a lot fewer spider webs than the first time I had transversed the interior. I never could get used to the damp and pungent smell inside there. But the closer we got to the opening the cleaner the air started to smell. In fact with the door ajar below, the air formed a current up and out of the opening at the top. I popped out of the hole and crawled on the planks over to the ladder that went up to the catwalk and then on up to the top of the tower.

Alden had just appeared in the trap door when I noticed several kids over in Solberg's front yard. They were waving to us. Of course, we waved back to them. I noticed Faye Solberg in the group. I never had told anyone but I thought she was just about as nice as she could be. In fact, I was suddenly and uncontrollably overcome with the desire to show off at that altitude because she was there watching.

The tower had one inch steel rods running from one leg to it's neighbor supporting the entire structure. The rods formed a giant Ex on every side of the legs. They went half way up the structure and were repeated on the second half. One of the rods was within my reach where I stood on the plank platform. Totally out of my head with some kind of crazy foolhardiness I didn't understand, I reached both hands up and grabbed the rod. I swung out over the open space down below and came back and landed where my feet had started. I let go with one hand and waved to the kids in the front yard. Alden said, "What the Heck are you doing?"

I replied, "Going up to the catwalk!"

Once we were both on the catwalk, we were waving to our admiring friends on the ground. Alden said, "Well, I'm going on up to the top." And with that he took hold of the ladder that lead to the top. This ladder was different than the one attached to the leg. It was made of two inch steel about 3/8 of an inch thick and was connected to the catwalk on the bottom and went up and over and out of sight on the roof of the tower. I said, "Okay! I'm with you." Alden began to climb.

When he got about a third of the way up, I got on the ladder to start my ascent. It was then I felt a slight tremor in the ladder. Looking up, I saw Alden at the half way point, not moving. He was totally still. Then I noticed he was starting to shake. "Alden, what are you doing?"

"I can't move!"

"Alden! You have to move. Either go up or come down. You can't just stay there."

"I'm really scared, Larry! I can't seem to let go to climb!"

"Okay, just come on down. One step at a time. Move a foot, and then move a hand. You can do it!"

Slowly he began to come back down the ladder. I was waiting for him on the catwalk. When he finally got to the catwalk, he didn't stop. He said, "I'm going down on the inside. I'll see you on the ground."

I waited until he was out of sight inside the housing. It was at this time I was attracted to the sound of someone yelling to me. I thought it was the kids on the ground. I looked over the edge of the catwalk and waved at the Policeman that was waving frantically at me. Boy oh boy! How dumb! I guess I'd better come down and face the music. At least Alden was safe on the inside of the housing.

The policeman was not what I would call courteous. He demanded to know what I thought I was doing and why I was doing it. My answer sums up the reasons most kids do dumb stuff, "I don't know!"

He took me in his squad car and delivered me to my home. Unknown to me, the Lutheran Minister and his wife were paying a pastoral call on mom and dad when the policeman rang the front doorbell. Upon telling my mom and dad what I had been caught doing of course my dad queried, "And what in the world did you think you were doing?"

Once again I uttered that most famous pre-teen/teenage reason. "I don't know!"

The pastor and his wife said something to the effect, "Well, we really need to be getting along. It's been very nice visiting with you Francis and Beulah. We must do it again soon." And out the door they vanished. ***Poof!***

The sheriff, assuming an informative tone, said, "You know, Francis, there is actually a fine associated with unauthorized trespassing on the water tower. Since your boy, Larry, here has a good record and this is his first offense, I'll just take it upon myself to not make a note of this infraction. I do have to say that if it were to happen again, you would have to pay a pretty stiff fine. You get what I mean."

Dad answered, "Oh, I don't think you have to ever worry about that happening again." Those words were accompanied by a look I'll remember for the rest of my life. All I could do was nod a very definite assent.

After the police car drove away, I overheard dad say to mom, "You'd think that they would have more important stuff to do than chase kids off the water tower." I don't think I was supposed to hear that comment.

And thus ended all of my tower escapades!!!

Isn't it interesting how ideas of acceptable behavior change with passing time? Growing up in the 1950s there were entirely contrary customs and mores considering saying and doing what today would be considered outlandishly politically incorrect but in the day seemed perfectly innocent. I offer the following as an example. L

Howard Robinson and the Trampoline Caper

Isn't it interesting that so often some people just stand out from the crowd? Whether it's a guy or a gal, they just stand out. They just look great no matter what they do and are naturally friendly. It has nothing to do with the dollar worth of their parents. In fact, some times family fortune is a misfortune for the kids. Howard Robinson (Howie) would certainly be one of the fortunate ones.

He always had a joke about old Aunt Tillie (I made up the name) that was just a little questionable as to propriety. Amoungst guys it was okay, but for mixed company…. His car was a little older (about a 1946 Chevy with a sloping back), dark color, maybe black, was famous for being able to hold 10 or more kids at once. One of my readers confessed that she had been in the car when it had been stopped by the cop. Another, Bob Zuck, told that the cop had said, "Well, Howard

Robinson, you have too many kids in your car. It is overloaded." To which Howard had replied, "We only have 3 in the front seat so we should be okay."

The officer had been stuck for an answer until he glanced in the back seat. "How about the eight kids in the back, including the ones on the bottom under the feet of the ones on top? You know what? I think you need a bigger car!"

Scobey was Crazed about sports. Back in the day we had Football for the boys, then Basketball for the boys, then in the Summer we had American Legion Baseball for the boys. The girls had Home Ec and Cheering. Music in the High School under the direction of Art Brandvold, was a favorite for boys and girls. We had a big band and Chorus.

It was into this plethora of athleticism that the school acquired a full sized trampoline. We all got to try a little bit but I got the feeling that the coaches were looking for a student with the right stuff. When I gave it a try, I thought it was kinda okay but I was a dedicated Trumpet player. No split lip on the edge of the trampoline for me.

Howard was born to the trampoline. They started him out with a belt around the waist (probably a whole body belt) with ropes up to the ceiling and down to two handlers. It wasn't long before Howie was out of the belt and doing his jumping and twirling and somersaulting to and fro sans belt. They always had "Catchers" near the apparatus but good luck to them if they had to catch him.

Each night that we had a "Home" basketball game there would be a double header. The "B" team would play the visitor's "B" team and then after that the band started playing between the games followed by the playing of the National Anthem, the presentation of the colors with hands over the hearts. (Everyone put their hand over their heart. Even old Codgers!) Then after a warm up the "A" squads took the hardwoods and played to the half. The last night of the home season the halftime entertainment was Howie on the Trampoline. My word, he did look great in the white gymnast suit. Every eye in the house was on him and you could hear a pin drop. He looped, hopped, re-looped, somersaulted, forward, backward and everything you could imagine. When he dismounted and took his final bow the thunderous applause shook the gym.

Later he confided in me that his name had been placed in the hat for "The Entertainer" for the half time of the Championship Game at the District Basketball Tournament held in Wolf Point, Montana. He didn't know if he was up to it or not. "Oh, you're up to it, alright. Heck, you'll steal the show. People won't even remember who won the game."

His old black car with the sloped rear end putted up and down the main street of Scobey. Down to the railroad track on the North end of the street and back up to the Dairy-O (?) across from the John Deere company on the East side. Then back down the street hoping to catch the eye of a girl or two and yet secretly hoping against it. I mean what if one of them said yes to a ride?

<u>The Tournament in Wolf Point</u>

The tournament in Wolf Point was a major event in the lives of High School kids in all the participating towns around. School was let out early on Thursday so the students who wanted to could drive the 50 or so miles and see the first games on that night. Then they could stay over Thursday night and Friday night and come back home on Saturday night or Sunday morning. As I remember it, six of us decided to stay over together at a motel in one room. (Poor room) There was always someone in charge of getting some beer for the group. We all pitched in some money and if we were lucky enough, we had some beer to drink. Otherwise it would be Pepsi for me. (Not Coke)

The time had drawn down to Saturday morning of the big game. Howie, a couple of other guys and I decided to go down town to see what was happening. When we got to the J.C.Penny's Store, Howie turned to us and said, "Hey guys! You see that clerk in the store right there? I'm going to go in and do my ***"Gimp"*** on him to sell me a new sports coat. Howie could imitate a person who was horribly crippled and never break a smile. (He would hunch up his right shoulder, bring his wrist to his shoulder, and nearly dislocate his hand with disfigured fingers and all. Along with this he would kind of snivel and speak unintelligibly.) In the meantime you guys sneak in after I'm with the clerk and from across the store start making fun of me. Let's see how the clerk handles it.

We watched as Howie kind of hobbled his way over to the clerk. We could see him saying something like, "Could you help me?"

We entered the store, making it to within a couple aisles and started our horrible teasing remarks.

The clerk was aghast at our behavior. "I can have those young ruffians removed from the store."

Howard in reply said, "Oh, that's okay. You get kind of used to it, you know."

The clerk, even more insistant said, "You over there! You stop that this instant!"

Of course we just got louder and more abusive. The clerk dropped all pretense of helping Howie and started advancing rapidly in our direction. Of course we ran out the door laughing. In the meantime Howie had hobbled out to the sidewalk and left with us, leaving the poor clerk totally befuddled.

OH, DID WE THINK WE HAD FUN!!!
That night at the halftime of the big game Howie was the entertainment. We waited outside the dressing room (locker room) for him to come out and we would accompany him to the gym where the trampoline was

center circle. As we got to the door into the gym who was taking tickets? You guessed it. THE CLERK from J.C.Penny's.

He looked with furrowed brow at Howie in his performance outfit, perfect in body and in total control physically. He spoke, "Don't I know you from somewhere?"

Howie, looking away, breezed, "Don't think so!" and he was off to the performance of a lifetime. We coughed a couple times, looking away, handed the fellow our tickets and went in, still chuckling about our prank of that afternoon.

The Back Seat With Myrna

The year was 1957. I was 17 years old, a Junior in High School, an avid fan of Johnny Unitas, the Brooklyn Dodgers, Elvis Presley, Chesterfield cigarettes, Lawrence Welk, Pepsi (not Coke), Mars Bars, Chocolate Chip Cookies, playing guitar and singing old Country Songs in Harry Chornuck's Nash Rambler, rotation pool down at Hackman's pool hall, and most of all dragging Scobey's main street in my 1951 Pontiac Sedan (complete with sun visor, flat head eight, and an automatic cigarette dispenser/lighter). While not having a lot of close personal friends, I did have a nice number of what I call "run around together and have a good time" friends. Somehow, thus far, I had managed to avoid the "Tender Trap" Frank Sinatra was singing about. That was about to change forever.

It was time for the District High School Music Festival. This year it was being held in Glasgow, Montana. Mr. Art Brandvold, our music teacher had managed to put together an incredible band and chorus in our small town. He took all the students in the two groups to the festival. It was a large undertaking for him, his wife and the parent chaperons. All the solo and Ensemble performers were adjudicated on Friday, during the day and all the large ensembles, (Band and Chorus) were judged on Saturday. Then Saturday evening the best band and the best chorus and the best ensembles performed a concert along with the massed band.

After performing in a vocal octet and a trumpet trio on Friday, I was at loose ends as were several of my friends. John, whose folks had a nice big Cadillac, suggested we triple date at the drive-in movie that evening. I thought it sounded like a capital idea. Just think, a drive-in in a big strange town, a big beautiful auto, a girl (I had been having some less than pure thoughts about my trumpet partner Myrna), a nice dark night…

 John was driving. He was with a girl up front. Even though the car was large, fitting four teenagers into the back seat was a bit of a trick. Myrna and I were on the right side and the other couple were on our left. We laughed and joked our way into the large speaker-littered lot at the drive-in. The light in the sky had not yet totally gone and so the picture on the screen was a little dim. Once we got our pop corn, drinks and milk duds we were set for the show.

I quite honestly am unable to tell you the name of that movie today. In fact, I couldn't have told you the next day. It is true that best laid plans of mice and men often go astray. I hadn't been able to think of anything but Myrna since John suggested the movie. How I ever got up the guts to ask her I have no idea. But now here we were. Crowded together in the back seat in the dark.

How in the world do I go about doing what the older boys had talked so freely about in the locker room? What to do? How to get started?

Slowly I stretched my arms out in a big yawn (my right elbow coming down on the padding behind Myrna's head). Ah…part way there. She couldn't possibly suspect anything. My dastardly plan was in motion. Ever so slowly my hand stole toward her short cut hair. Soon I would be touching her on the top of the head. My God!!! I wondered if she could hear my heart doing the "Thumper the Rabbit Act".

Now for the highlight of the evening. Slowly, I began to extend the right side of my neck towards hers. It wasn't far now. Just a little bit more. My esophagus felt as though it was being forced out of shape. About the time I thought I wouldn't be able to continue my quest, our necks touched. Ahh…The electric shock of our ultimate intimacy. Our necks touching as I patted her softly on her head. What a glorious way to spend an evening.

Soon the movie was over and we returned to the motel where Mr. "B" had put us up overnight. When we drove up the whole world came unglued. All the adults in the chaperone party had already had kittens and I believe one or two had delivered cows—hysteria reigned. We hadn't told anyone where we were going. That was a big mistake. We all were severely reprimanded and sent to our beds facing criminal charges the following day.

I personally thought it was well worth it. The next day when all the guys asked what had taken place in the car, I simply told them, "Oh, nothing much. You know, we necked, we petted."

DON KENSKA REAL TEACHER!!!

<u>OPENING DAY</u>

As a High School student I was at best mediocre. My parents didn't press me for high grades. I viewed school in general as something I had to put up with until I was finished. I did work in the Music Department. I enjoyed playing my cornet and my guitar. In those days (the Fifties) there was no big push on to develop a class of overly smart people with brains bigger than their ability to get along with their fellow human beings. We treated Elementary and High School as a place one could get an introduction to many different kinds of subject matter and make a somewhat informed choice about what one would care to pursue as a vocation. If you wanted to go to college upon graduation, all you had to do was apply to any of the state colleges and you would be accepted as a Freshman in the fall. If you flunked out of High School or didn't take some of the "meatier" classes well then...

I kind of enjoyed High School, finding it a rather relaxed and occasionally an interesting way to spend ones time, growing up. As long as I didn't get an "F", I was okay. I didn't know what they would do if you did flunk a class. Would you have to repeat it? I didn't know anyone that had it happen. All I knew was that I didn't want to be the one to find out the hard way. Besides, talking with my folks, I decided to go to college after graduation. The people at the school had told us I should take what was considered a "college prep" series of classes. So as a Senior, I found myself enrolling in the Chemistry class taught by Mr. Don Kenska.

Mr. Kenska was the kind of teacher I liked. He didn't try to be popular with the kids. He was all about his subject matter and preparing kids for college. The school had a rule that if you got an "A" during the semester, you didn't have to take the semester final in that class. Of course, Mr. Kenska followed that rule, but he encouraged all the students, including the "A" students to take the two hour final test so you could get ready for the major tests you would have to take in college. Most of the kids took the finals even though they may have qualified to opt out. He always tried his best to treat kids equally no matter what.

All the students were waiting outside the Chem Lab door, waiting for the bell to ring in the first day of a year filled with CHEMISTRY! Of course all the kids who wanted to be as close to the teacher as possible, were first in line. We knew that seats would be assigned by first come, first served. I chose a spot back a ways in the line. It was always difficult for me to differentiate between the ones who liked being close to the teacher for "points" and those who were simply near sighted. Of course they have glasses for myopia, soooo...

Kenska was a new teacher when I first had him in Physics, as a Junior. Now as a Senior, I was back again in his Chem class. Wanting to excite and interest all the kids in class the first day of Chemistry he arranged to show a demonstration experiment called Mount Vesuvius. He sat a graduated narrow neck flask on the lab desk in the front row. Oh my, how the students leaned in to watch every move he made. He explained,"Now then, this flask has a little quantity of water, H2O, in the bottom, as you can see. In this jar we have the metal Sodium, Na. You know how water puts fires out...I think you'll be amazed what happens when I place this small quantity of Sodium in the flask of water. All right everyone. Gather round. This is what is going to be happening in this class for an entire year!"

With that being said, he dropped the piece of Sodium into the water flask. As everyone leaned in to observe the unique interaction between these two chemical substances, there began a kind of sizzling sound and the Sodium was moving on its own. The awed silence of the room was broken with the "BANG!!!" of a cherry bomb as the flask disintegrated into one thousand seventy two extremely small glass shards sending a mixture of glass, water and burning sodium throughout the room. Startled as I was, I felt fortunate not to have been one of the "Myopes". I smiled. Those that needed it were sent to the lavatory. (I never did see any lava down there.) The rest were told to sit down and listen to learn what had happened.

I don't recall any fatalities from the experience, however the class had six fewer students from there on out. (You could count them "Fatalities of Fear").

THE REFINING EXPERIENCE

Since my time in First Grade I have noticed that occasionally I have a tendency to allow my mind to wander. I have had the amazing ability to be interested in something and suddenly find myself five hundred thirty one and a half miles away, on a grassy knoll, watching a cavalcade drive past with VIPs in the cars. WOW! Who is that in that Cadillac Convertible? Different teachers have treated me differently. Some act as though I personally insulted them. Some, on the other hand seem to understand that I don't have complete control over what my mind does. Mr. Kenska was, for the most part fairly understanding.

The entire Senior Class took a trip from our little outpost of Scobey, Montana to the big city of Billings, Montana. The overall idea was to take these students on a trip to broaden their horizons. We were scheduled to make a stop at Roundup, Montana to go down in the Coal Mines there, an interesting experience. After that we wound up in Billings at the Northern Hotel where we would stay for two nights. We were then scheduled to tour the campus of Eastern Montana College of Education where we saw class rooms, dormatories, the

Student Union, the book store, and were introduced to a variety of teachers, administrators and a few select students. The next day we visited the working Cenex Refinery in Laurel, Montana. After that we wrapped our bus around us and went home. It was a mind opening experience. Thank you Mr. Kenska.

In preparation for the trip to the refinery, Mr. Kenska had the refinery in Laurel send him a large sample of crude oil. The class lesson was intended to teach us about the refining process. As he always did, he handled the crude with great care, parceling it out into relatively large mouth test tubes so that each student could have an equal quantity of their own. When I got my test tube I noticed it didn't quite fit in my normal test tube rack. I held it up. I twirled and swirled it. It was the nastiest stuff I could recall ever seeing. It was thick, mucky, ugly, brownish stuff that belonged in the toilet. It even smelled like the toilet would make a great final resting place for it. It was time for Mr. Kenska to give us the final instructions for conducting the experiment.

The purpose of the first step in the process was to thin the muck down by gradually heating it in the tube. Mr. Keska cautioned us, "Now, as we heat the oil in the tubes you will notice it beginning to bubble. We all have to keep constantly moving the tubes so the heat is applied evenly from top to bottom. Don't allow the tube to remain in one spot for too long." We lit our Bunsen burners and holding the test tubes of oil with the spring loaded tube holders, we proceeded to introduce them to the flame.

At first, I found it very interesting to watch the oil react to the heat of the lamp. It was at this time that the foul odor of Centuries Dead Dinosaurs began to permeate the room. I studiously continued with the instructed movement of the tube in the flame. Slowly the smell redirected my conscious thought to the memory of the time my friend Alden and his younger brother, Clive, and I hiked out to the "S" hill for an overnight camp out. We had heated two or three cans of Campbell's Pork and Beans for supper. Apparently, one of my co-campers had a not to friendly reaction to the beans and in the middle of the night had awakened everyone with the extremely foul odor of Beans-Gone-Wrong, an ancient Chinese curse, so I've heard. As I reflected on the memory, I had forgotten to keep the test tube moving as per the instruction. I had stopped on the exact bottom of the tube. Unknown to me things were about to happen I could not have predicted in a thousand years.

Suddenly, I was startled into reality by the test tube giving a surprisingly violent recoil and as I watched I heard an audible "Kaa-pluuff" from it. To my dismay I saw the entire contents of my tube take off with the speed of sound. Out of the tube, into the air, it was on its way to the front of the class room. In horror, I watched as time began to stand still. The glob of gook was now inching its way in painful sloth, towards Mr. Kenska at the board in front of the class. Should I shout a warning? What could I do? In his meticulously starched and ironed white lab coat, his right hand suspended up to the chalkboard, he was about to become the victim of a per-historic nasty unintentional graffiti attack. As quickly as the message from my test tube slowed, it assumed lightning speed and arrived squarely on target getting Mr. Kenska and his coat totally plastered from right hand all the way down across his back.

All the class went totally silent. Without moving a muscle or even turning his head I heard him say, "BRASEN?"

Apparently Mr. Kenska forgave me because he allowed me to go on the big trip to Billings.

CHLORINE GAS PRODUCTION

I suppose in every Chemistry Class there has to be an experiment that includes producing Chlorine Gas. As you all know, Chlorine Gas is deadly for humans. It was used by the Axis Forces in the Trench Warfare of WWI. I'm not sure I understand why it is necessary for high school students to create the stuff. Non the less...Here we go.

"Okay, students,"began Mr. Kenska, "today we are going to produce Chlorine gas! Now you need to remember, this gas is poisonous." We filled our receptor beaker with water and placed it upside down in our trays filled with water. Next, we attached a flexible hose to the black, one-holed stopper for our test tubes and placed the end of the hose under the upside down, water filled beaker.

Mr. Kenska asked, "Is everyone ready?" Pause… "Good. Now place the Hydrochloric Acid in the test tube." Pause… "Good, now carefully drop the piece of metal into the acid and place the stopper on the tube." Everyone did just as he said. "Now, observe the Chlorine gas displacing the water in the beaker. Note the greenish tinge to the gas."

The same thing began to happen at all twenty eight lab stations at the same time. My beaker filled to capacity and the gas started filling the tray the water was in. It was really cool! It ran over the tray and spilled out onto the lab table. Backing a little away, I said, "Hey, this stuff is rolling right off my table and down onto the floor."

"Oh, my God!" from Mr. Kenska. "Quick, everyone flush the tube mixture down the drain. You in the back, get the windows open. Everybody get to a window and breath fresh air."

Edna Mae said, "I don't feel so good."

"Go to the nurse. Wanda, you go with her and report back to me."

Of course, she was one of the students that sat as close to the front as she could. I think that she got a touch more exposure than some of us seated further back.

"Everyone, take a good whiff of this ammonia. It will counteract the Chlorine."

All the kids were quite concerned when Edna Mae didn't return to school the next day. She did make it back the day after that, but we all thought she was moving kind of slow. In the end we all did survive the Chlorine Event. I believe we all came out of it unharmed.

I would not be surprised to learn that Mr. Kenska spent many a late night before "Lab Days" making sure of his experiments after that.

THE POINT OF CRYSTALLIZATION

It is now April of 1958 and I have been eighteen years old for about a month. In Chemistry Class Mr. Kenska is reviewing a chapter in the book in preparation for a chapter exam. Question7 on page 142. Okay Carl, you got that one? Let's see, question 8, same page. Lorraine, how about you? And so it goes… I glanced out the window and noticed it had started to snow. Gosh, it looked just like the weather did when I was out in the country with Barry Handy, visiting his hand made trapper's dugout he used for staying overnight while processing muskrat furs. I remember you had to crawl in on hands and knees and make a sharp turn to the left into a large underground room. All the boards he had put over the dugout and covered with dirt didn't let the cold or wind in. He had a little wood stove that more than heated the place. The low ceiling was just right if you sat on your hind end. There was an inch or two between your head and the boards above. "Hey, Finn. Put another log on the fire."

What's that sound. It sounds like someone is calling my name. "Larry, Larry." Who the heck knows I'm out here? I hear it again. "Larry, Mr. Brasen." This time louder and more insistent, followed by general laughter and nervous giggling. Suddenly I snap back to reality...Chemistry Class...My Name...Mr. Kenska...Oh, Crap..."I'm sorry Mr. Kenska", head shaking, "what was that again?"

"Question number eleven."

I look down at my book. There is no question eleven on the page. In desperation I turn the page. No question eleven there either!

"I'm really sorry, what page are we on?"

DEAD SILENCE! "Larry, I'm afraid I just can't continue to have you in my class. I've tried to work with you for over half a year and nothing I do seems to make a dent. As much as I hate to do this, I'm telling you to gather up your belongings. All of your material in the desk. All your notebooks. Leave all the equipment that belongs to the Chemistry Department in the drawers. Take your Chem book with you and report to the Principal's office. Tell him what happened here and ask him to reassign you to a different class and give him your book."

Not a sound...No student giggling...No nervous titter...No one breathing…

HEART POUNDING IN MY CHEST AND I N MY EARS!!! Breath coming shallow...Without this class how could I get into college? What would I tell my folks? Gathering my stuff took seventeen hours...loaded, I walk toward the door...slowly I reach my hand out to grasp the door knob… (You ever notice how a metal door handle feels cool to the touch?) As I touched the door knob an inspiration flashed in my mind! Turning in the most abject posture I could possibly assume, I said, "<u>Mr. Kenska, I really don't want to go!</u>"

He said, "Larry, do you think if I allowed you to remain in this class, you could pay attention and never get lost like that again for the remainder of the year?"

I replied, "Mr. Kenska, I promise. I'll <u>never</u> daydream in your class again."

"Larry, I know what a fine musician you are. I know how much you love your music. You just have to know that you need to perform in all your classes like you do for Mr. Brandvold." (Music Teacher)
"Now, would you like to return to your desk and rejoin the class?"

"Yes, sir, I would."

Epilogue: Fast forward to my class's 50th reunion. At Scobey's Pioneer Town, at the Dirty Shame Show, in the Olde Rex Theatre I played a trumpet solo with the pit band. In the audience was my old friend and mentor Mr. Don Kenska. Afterward, out in front of the theatre the cast members were doing a "Meet and Greet" with the audience. Over the years I had come to value Mr. Kenska as one of my very best teachers during high school. He walked boldly right to me and wrapped me in his arms and said, "Larry, I always knew you were going to make it in music. You were just great today."

I said, "Remember the time you almost threw me out of your class?"

He said, with just a hint of a smile, "Sometimes the best of us need a little shock."

Valier, Montana

Another great place to start teaching!

SMALL WORLD

Charles Van Gorden was my Senior Social Studies Teacher at Scobey, Montana High School. He was also the main Sports Coach in the High School. During my Senior year while passing from one class to another, Mr. Van Gordon stopped me in the hall and asked what I was going to do after graduation. That was about as close to counseling as we got back in Scobey in 1958. I told him I didn't have any plans really set for the next year.

"Well, what did you have in mind as far what kind of work you wanted to do?"

"To tell you the truth I hadn't really thought about it all that much", I replied, wishing I could get away and on to my next class.

"Did you have in mind farming with your Dad?", He asked.

Now he had my attention. As much as I admired my dad I knew I didn't want to be a farmer like him. I remembered the conversation dad and I had not too long before this as we were driving to town in the pickup after a day of summer fallowing. Speaking of the farming operation, he had said, "You know Larry, I haven't put all this together just for me and your mother. If you would like maybe when you graduate from High School we could figure out a way that you could come in with me as a partner and eventually buy me out and this could all be yours. Oops, be careful to keep the wheels in the tracks. These gravel roads can really throw you if you don't watch it. How does that sound to you?"

"Staying in the tracks" had been the bane of my life for as long as dad had allowed me to do the driving to the farm in the morning and back to town in the evening. I knew that I didn't want to spend my life dealing with **things**. I felt I had a calling to interact with **people**. So my answer was already fairly well formalized. "Dad, I don't know what I want to do for sure, but I'm sure I don't want to be a farmer. I want to deal with people."

I'm sure dad's reply to me was meant to be thought provoking. "Well, would you like to work at the grocery store for Mr. Getchel? Or how about the implement shop at Solbergs."

None of these options had appealed to me at all.

To Mr. Van Gorden's question I answered, "No. I want to work with people, not things."

"You know, you should consider being a teacher. I saw how you conducted the class the other day when I had the students be the teachers. You did a very professional job. Have you thought about going to Eastern Montana College of Education?"

At that particular time in my life I was totally consumed with the thought of successfully getting out of High School. The mere thought of any additional schooling was so repugnant that I nearly regurgitated on his shoes. "Oh, I don't think so Mr. Van Gordon," was the best I could come up with and I hurried off to my next class.

The next fall found me enrolling at Eastern Montana College as a "Pre-Business" major. I guess, after counseling with the college enrollment department my folks thought that the best thing they could enroll me in was "Pre-Business". This lasted the better part of three years. During that time I made friends with Music Majors and formed a jazz quartet named "The Moonglows". I met and married my wife, Betty. We both dropped out of College. We had our wonderful son, Larry Junior. We both re-enrolled at Eastern Montana College, with Betty majoring in Elementary Education and me majoring in Music Education K-12. Eventually, seven years after enrolling in college I had earned a degree, Betty earning hers the same quarter, we graduated together. Actually, we graduated in alphabetic order with Betty graduating before me.

Now it came time to go looking for teaching positions where we could both teach. You must realize that in Montana many of the school districts have only one Elementary, Middle school and High School. Because of this many of the districts made a rule banning the hiring of husband and wife in the same district. One district that didn't have such a rule was Valier, Montana. As a part of our whirlwind job seeking circuit we stopped in Valier and were interviewed by Bruce Milne. Mr. Milne was the Superintendent of the Valier Schools. After what seemed an exhaustive interview we were both issued teaching contracts for the next year. All we had to do was sign them and we were in. We still had appointments to look at two or three other schools so we asked for and were given three days in which to accept or return the contracts unsigned. We were excited as we drove away. This little town looked a lot like the small Montana farming/ranching communities in which we both had grown up, though time and distance now separated us from them. We felt we could fit in here quite nicely. The school buildings were relatively new and well kept. We were both favorably impressed with Mr. Milne. After interviewing at one or two other small towns and receiving contracts from them also we returned to our future home of Valier, Montana and gave them our signed contracts. We had our new life now in our hands.

Imagine my surprise when on the first day of school, from down the hall, I heard a familiar voice from my distant past saying, "Well, Larry Brasen. Welcome to Valier."

"Mr. Van Gorden!" My new High School Principal.

"You can call me Chuck now Larry."

Battle Hymn

We approached Valier, Montana from the East. We'd driven through Great Falls, North through Conrad and eventually turned West. One of the things we noticed right away were the wind breaks made of trees and hedges on the West side of all the farm locations. The wind buffeted the car severely- sometimes actually slowing us down. We could see the town of Valier from some distance perched on the flat, rolling hills of the countryside.

Betty, "You can really see forever out here, can't you?"

We had accepted our first teaching contracts together. Betty was to be teaching a 1st - 2nd split class and I would be teaching all the music classes in the Elementary, Jr. High and High School and 2 sections of Freshman Earth Science. Larry Jr. would attend kindergarten and then stay with Karen Dunlap and her two kids until we were all done with the school day. We were set for our first year in Valier.

After the first few weeks of "Mr. Previous did it this way", the kids finally decided I might know what I was doing and I decided the kids were just about as nice as they could be. These were fresh country kids mostly from the farms surrounding the small Montana town. A few of the students lived in town and it seemed that all of them had cars that were quite a bit nicer than our old Ford Falcon and my own pet, the Kaiser. The townspeople were the friendliest group of people I believe I'd ever met. My theory was if you live where the wind constantly could blow you over if you didn't pay attention, you would have to learn to depend on each other and that might just include learning to be nice to each other.

The kids and I were busy preparing what was called the Christmas Concert. As the Semester ending concert approached we had everything pretty well planned out. The music was chosen, practiced, rehearsed, and we were ready. The one thing that I felt was missing was some kind of concert ending piece.

With little time left before the concert, Thanksgiving was upon us. We had decided to spend the four day recess in Harlowton, Montana with Betty's mother, Mary. We packed Larry Jr., the dog Prince, and Betty and me in the Falcon and drove over to central Montana. Parking in front of Betty's folks home, we got out, woke up Larry Jr. and got Prince out of the car and there was Mary dispensing the hugs and kisses and fried chicken she was famous for.

The next day it was T.V. Parade time. Then of course the incredible turkey feast. Later, we were back watching the televised football games when **it** happened. We were watching the half-time entertainment. Back then they showed the entertainment provided by the college bands without interruption by the sports casters or commercials. The band on the field performed "The Battle Hymn of the Republic". It was a simple piece performed with band and chorus. As the band formed different shapes on the field, the chorus sang the age old Civil War tune.

Suddenly, I could see the score written in front of my eyes. The concept was born complete. All I had to do was take dictation. It starts with the percussion. The snare drums—one, two, three, four. Add the tuba on fundamental single low tones with the solo flute over the top on the melody. My mind was racing.

I sat at Mary's classy little parlor piano purchased years before from Johnny and Selma Peterson at Lindamood's Music on 28th Street in downtown Billings. I started picking out the melody and the chords. I began to hear each part of the band as it was added. Make a gradual build up adding each section until every instrument was playing ending with a grand huge chord and then bringing the chorus in at the beginning of the first verse. End the piece with a series of three tonic chords over the chorus holding the last note and then off.

We left early Sunday morning and were back home in Valier by mid-afternoon. I went directly to the school. In my office was the staff paper I needed for writing the score. If I were to arrange this piece and teach it to the kids, I needed to get started yesterday. Returning home hours later, I brought the rough score of "The Battle Hymn". I found all the words and piano part in a community hymnal forgotten on my shelf of dusty books.

My trusty Royal portable typewriter hummed the words onto the purple ditto copy original. By the time School started I had been up all night. Chuck, Ed, Jack and the guys in the teacher's lounge took one look at me and Jack said, "You look like you could use a cup of this tar. Where ya been?"

I produced the completed score and all the purple originals of the words and announced, "I've been up all night working on the <u>Battle Hymn of the Republic</u>."

The talk immediately turned to the sports results from the long weekend.

Now, before the band could get the music, each part had to be written individually. I started the arduous task of transposing and transcribing each part for each instrument. Since all the band students were going to take part, I wrote simple parts for beginners and more complex parts for the Seniors in High School. When all was totaled there were nearly thirty parts that had to be written.

During this marathon of copying band parts, the chorus and General Music classes were beginning practice on the singing portions. Each class, including the 1st Grade on up, was assigned a part of a verse. As they practiced in class I became more excited. They all began to follow my example and the entire town was abuzz with the excitement generated from the school.

"I hear you're going to be doing <u>The Battle Hymn</u>."

Smiling, "Ya. I'm really excited. Should be darn good."

By Wednesday morning each band part had been transcribed. There was one copy of each. Now copies of each part had to be made. Members of the High School Band who were also members of the chorus were interested in taking part in the copying process. We met after school in the multi-purpose room and on the floor and available desks and tables were spread out all the originals that needed to be copied. By Thursday morning during band classes we began to practice the piece. I could see that it was going to work and called for a meeting of all Band and Chorus and General Music students that could make it after lunch in the multi-purpose room on Friday.

The room was noisy. There were band students on the stage and kids lounging all over the multi-purpose room. I was sure that Carl, the janitor, was looking my way with a slight frown that said, "I know who's going to have to clean this all up later." Everyone got quiet when I blew the whistle.

"O.K. Band kids on the stage start the intro."

Just as I had planned the Band began the familiar old tune bringing the introduction to an end. Then the kids standing all over the room started singing their parts. Soon the room was filling up with students and teachers that were not even part of the program. Now the band and chorus were singing together. As the music came to its climactic end Bruce Milne, the Superintendent, came bursting in.

Very excited, "Do you know what you have here,
Larry?"

"What do you mean?"

"This is great! Are you going to do this for the
Christmas program?"

"That was my intention. Why?"

"My god! Come and see me in my office after school
as soon as you can. O.K.?"

"Sure."

Once in Bruce's office, he loosened his tie and asked,
"What else are you planning for the program coming
up?"

I excused myself and stepped across the hall to my
room and retrieved the rough draft program. He took a
long look at it and then asked, "Now what kind of piece
is this <u>Panis Angelicus</u>?"

It is a religious piece by Mozart.

"Religious. O.K. What if we made a three pointed
Gothic Arch with the three intertwining circles and
crosses as a back drop? Then we could start with the
Chorus in place, open the curtain, and there would be
one solitary candle, burning on the piano. That would
focus the audience's attention and then as the piano and
the chorus begin to make music, the colored lights would

slowly begin to rise. As the music fades away at the end we'll bring the lights all back down to the single candle still burning on the stage. At the exact time the music ends, the curtain closes on the dark stage. What do you think?"

All I could manage was a rather stunned, "Gosh." Then, "Where will we get all the lights. Where will we get the backdrop?"

"Don't you worry about that. I'll take care of all that. You just make the music the best it has ever been. Now, about the Battle Hymn. How do you see this being presented?"

"Gee, I really don't know. I hadn't thought about the presentation. I've just been busy writing and transposing and teaching."

Leaning forward in an almost confidential pose, "Larry, who do you think you're competing with? It is no longer enough to just stand your groups up in front of their adoring parents and have them perform. Every day all of the public is inundated with the most accomplished performers the world has ever produced. T.V. has become your standard of excellence. You have a choice--do the standard presentation and receive standard results or attempt a professional presentation

and take your chances on how you will be received."
Leaning back in his office chair, he smiled, "What do
you think?"

These thoughts were all new to me. He seemed
to know what he was talking about. "So, what do I need
to do?"

"Larry, I have an idea for the <u>Battle Hymn</u>." He
began to draw sketches on blank paper on his desk. "We
can make platforms of varying size and height. Some
will be 2 feet tall and 4 X 8. Some will be 1 foot tall and
4 X 8. Some will be 1 foot tall and 2 X 8. See how
these can be used on the stage to create different and
interesting tableaus? We can put the band on the stage in
a grand triangle like a pyramid. We can place all the
singers on risers in front of the stage spilling off to create
the base of the pyramid. We can roll red, white and blue
strips of foot wide cheese cloth up on a long 1 X 2 and
suspend it from the ceiling behind the band. Just as the
piece reaches its climax we'll let the red white and blue
banner go. Maybe we could march out the American
flag at the same time. What do you think?"

Dizzy, I asked, "Where does all this equipment
come from? We don't have much time to put this all
together."

"Don't worry. The lights are already in place. We just need to run the wires to them and hook them up. I know that I can talk to Jack out in the shop and he can begin to manufacture the wooden platforms."

The next days rolled by. I visited the shop and was interested to see the pieces for the platforms being cut out of plywood. Talking with my friend, Jack Dunlap, I found out that he took the assembly line approach to this project. With a week left before the performance the platforms began rolling out of the shop and onto the stage. It was truly amazing! Every ten minutes or so a new platform would be brought into the multi-purpose room. Jack really knew his business.

On Tuesday evening, with three days remaining until the concert a crew of electricians appeared on stage. Using dish soap and elbow grease all the wires were pulled through the conduit which was already in place. In short order we were able to flip the lights on and off or do a slow brighten and dim. Colored gel magically appeared and was placed in the appropriate fixtures.

The stage was ready. The question was, was I? With all the added expense and intensive interest I began to have some doubts about my ability to pull this whole thing off. The program had grown to such importance in

my mind that I could think of nothing else. I alone knew
of my inexperience. Never in my life had I written any
piece of music for band and chorus. Never in my life
had I participated in a musical presentation of this kind.
True, I had been in some plays in High School. They
required special sets. I couldn't remember ever taking
part in something this overwhelming. It seemed to be on
everyone's lips. When Betty and Larry Jr. and I went out
for pizza at the Lighthouse on Lake Francis, people there
would ask how everything was coming. I couldn't get
away from it - it had taken on a life of its own. If it
didn't fly, I was going to have to dig a hole somewhere
out in those vast grain fields and just pull the stubble in
over me.

The night of the big program was upon us. The
multi-purpose room was filled to overflowing. The
sound of excited people bubbled out of the two main
doors into the hall. (Many of the former students who
were away at college were back home for the holidays.)
Grandparents and Uncles and Aunts and Cousins from
some distance were in the crowd. People who had no
relatives in the program at all attended. I'm betting that
the bars downtown were wondering where everyone
was. The lights dimmed and came back up, warning the

audience the show was about to begin. Up on the stage behind the closed curtain the chorus was quietly waiting for the opening number. The single candle was lighted. All the stage lights were off. The chorus and I stood with heads bowed. The backdrop was just visible in the candle light. At the nod of my head the curtain opened. The audience was totally hushed. Even little babies knew that something special was taking place and were quiet. The piano began its introduction with Ramona Arnst at the keys. Slowly, as the intro was closing, the chorus brought their heads up and opened their eyes. That was the beginning of <u>Panis Angelicus</u>. Each piece we presented that night had the flavor of that indefinable something special and each was well received. Then it was time for <u>The Battle Hymn of the Republic</u>.

With the curtains closed, the band reassembled the platforms in the huge pyramid Bruce had imagined. All the band members were in place and the chorus members were walking on from the hallway onto the risers in front of the stage and on the stage right and left in front of the curtain on the apron. All the students in grades 1 through 6 were in the chorus or part of the extended band. There were even a few high school students who weren't members of the regular chorus who volunteered to be a part of the massed chorus. When everyone was in place the lights were turned down again in the audience and I stepped from the hallway to the front of the chorus. At my signal the curtains opened and the lights gradually came up to reveal the pyramid of kids. Before anything more could be done the audience burst into enthusiastic applause. Just the sight of all the students and the special lengths to which we had gone overwhelmed them.

All quiet.

"Ladies and gentlemen. Tonight we would like to dedicate this concert and particularly this final number to all the men and women serving in our armed forces who are unable to be with us here tonight either because they are too far distant or because they gave their lives so that we may be assembled here on this joyous occasion.

All quiet again.

The first snare drum--just as I had heard it in my mind. The tuba and flute duet. Now the reeds enter with the melody. Now the brass join in. Now the final Major chord of the introduction. Silence. The piano and the chorus begin. "Mine eyes have seen the glory of the coming of the Lord. He is trampling out the vintage where the grapes of wrath are stored... ." Now little by little the band joins in creating those beautifully strong chords under the words. Class by class, we progress. Now the final verse. "In the beauty of the lilies Christ was born across the sea. With a beauty in his bosom that transfigures you and me." Building power---"As He died to make men holy let us live to make men free"--- CRESCENDO---"His truth is marching on." Now full band---Trumpets in triplets on a chord---Trombones on ascending scale patterns from low to high and over---Sax section on the melody in three part harmony---Clarinets and Flutes on descending scale patterns---tympani repeating over and over and over that triplet pattern echoing the trumpets, "Glory, glory halleluja. Glory, glory halleluja." Down comes the red, white and blue streamers, and out onto the stage a Boy Scout marches the American flag. The music is deafening as it crashes toward the inevitable end. Hold the last word, "On" while the band plays its final three tonic chords and then silence.

Not a sound from the audience. Nothing. In all the world there was not a sound. What could be wrong? I stumbled out of the dead room seeking solace in the empty hall. What had happened? Then with the sound of one person beginning to clap, all the thunder of applause came pouring out. People laughing, people crying, some standing, some sitting in wonder, the audience began to pour out of the room into the hall where I was standing. The town blacksmith who was big and very strong came running at me. I didn't know what to expect. Wrapping his huge arms around me and with tears openly streaming down his face all he could do was say, "Thank you. Thank you. Thank you." His son was serving duty in a place not too many had even heard of named Viet Nam - I would never be the same.

Because of our rather restless natures, Betty and I moved from one job location to another several times. For some reason we did not keep in touch with any of our friends in Valier. However, no matter where I've gone, I've always taken a part of Valier, Montana with me. I know that I received much more from that town and the people than I gave. I learned more from Bruce Milne in one hour than I learned from all the previous education courses I had taken.

EPILOG

Over thirty years passed. It was my first year of teaching music in Roberts, Montana. As a member of the Tri-County Honor Band my students met with students from several other small schools to form a special traveling organization none of our schools could have individually put together. In a meeting of the directors, who I hadn't had the chance to get to know, the Band Director from Huntley Project, Montana said, "Have any of you folks ever heard of little town named Valier, Montana? I'm going to share a story with you that demonstrates the power of a music program to positively affect a community." He told my story!

GOOSE HUNTING

<u>Pep Band for the Thin Clads</u>

One of the responsibilities of the music teacher in Valier was to have a pep band at each of the home basketball games. I should really spell basketball with capital letters because, in that part of Montana, basketball was "King". Within a radius of about 40 miles from our little town were three of the biggest, most rabid, basketball towns in the whole state Class B conference. Even now when I hear the names of Conrad, Shelby, and Cut Bank, my basketball pulse goes up about 25 beats per minute. We were one of the smallest Class B schools in the state at the time and we had to compete with these giants. I thought we should be a Class C school. We would be playing schools that were much more our size. One problem with being a Class C school was the distance we would have to travel to compete. The other problem might have been that the pride of the community was at stake. It was almost as though they would rather lose in Class B than be true competitors in Class C. As a result of our classification, we lost a lot of games. In fact, my Pep Band played for a nearly unblemished record of losses for the three years I taught there.

After nearly half of our first Basketball season, my wife, Betty, our son Larry Jr., and I developed a pattern. First, on the evening of a home game, we would go to the school where I made sure there were once again enough kids to form a Pep Band. I would help them get set up on the little stage in the gym. Betty would do what she could to help and then she and Larry Jr. would go to the gym with their current books. Larry, at age 5, would be reading his favorite Golden Book of the day. Betty would then take up a position she found favorable and begin to read, knowing that before long people would come in, notice her by herself, and come over and instruct her in the latest community points of interest.

During the team warmup, the Pep Band would play a few tunes like the obligatory *Tequila*, followed by *The High Chaparral*, and then *Rock Around the Clock*, to name a few. At the beginning of the game we would play *The Star Spangled Banner* while the flag was marched out. Everyone in the room came to attention, placing their hands over their hearts, they would either stand in silence or join in the singing. Then we would watch helplessly as our team was slaughtered on the hardwood floor during the first half.

During half time, the Pep Band would continue to play for the supportive Band Parents that hadn't left for a smoke, coffee, pop, something stronger in the glove compartment, popcorn or just a visit with neighbors. With the beginning of the second half, the band could put away their horns, making an exodus across the far end of the basketball court, under the basket, heading to the music room. When everything was stowed, lights out, doors locked, we made our way back to the ongoing massacre.

Post-game Ritual

Following the game Betty, Larry Jr., and I would wind up over at Jack and Karen Dunlap's home. Jack was the head basketball coach for the school. Karen was, at the time, a Stay-at-home mom who had a babysitting service for all the teacher's pre-schoolers. That was where Larry Jr. stayed during the school day while Betty and I were teaching. We usually got there a little before Jack because it took him extra time to button up the sports facilities after the game. I would usually bring along a six pack of Rainier or Hamm's Beer and Betty would be sure to have some Coke or Pepsi. Their kids, Carolyn and Johnny and our Larry Junior, would play by themselves while we would just sit back and relax; Pop a beer, sing a song, talk about the game, cuss the general injustices in the world, play a word game that had dice with letters on the them and a miniature 3-minute hour glass, or whatever kind of R&R we could invent. That was how our rather unlikely friendship started.

Jack, a hulk of a man, would walk in the door with a smile that belied his true feelings about the game results. Popping a beer, he would fall heavily into a chair and sip the cool refreshment. "You know, Larry, it's about time to do some Goose hunting. You ever try it at all?"

"No, not really."

"I got a pit dug out in my friend's stubble field. If we left about four tomorrow morning we could get there and be covered up before the geese get up off the lake. You got a gun? Wanna try it?"

"Ya, I got a 12 gauge shotgun. Remington Pump. What kind of shells do you use?"

"Number 2 shot. I like em with the extra powder

for really reaching out there."

"You got any extra shells, Jack? We can't get em right now. It's too late."

"Ya, no problem. Ya wanna?"

"Ya, sounds like a fun."

"One thing. I don't like to have to wait for anyone because they sleep in. I'll drive up to your trailer and blink the lights a couple times. If you don't come on out, I'll just go on ahead without ya, O.K.?"

"Oh… yeah." Nodding, "O.K."

"Dress warm and ya might wanna bring some hot coffee or something along. It gets kinda cold out there just before the sun comes up."

The Quest

I awoke the next morning to some loud pounding on our trailer door. Crap! I overslept. Darting down the narrow aisle we called a hallway in my jockey shorts, I made it to the door just as Jack was turning to go. "Hey, come on in. I'll be right with ya. Let me just turn on my coffee and grab some clothes. Just a couple minutes."

Later in the pickup I noticed the chill in the air. "God, what is the temperature?"

"Well, It's just above freezing. These guys are only gonna be around here a little longer so today's the day."

Valier, Montana is out on the plains just miles from the Rocky Mountains of Glacier National Park. We always call them cardboard mountains because they just kind of appear out of nowhere. There are plains, and then mountains. Out on the flatlands away from the town, we could see the lights of Conrad, Shelby, and Cut Bank on a clear night. Each of these towns was easily 25 to 40 miles away. The wind came down the mountain slopes totally unimpeded. If there was just a strong breeze, we claimed the wind wasn't blowing. In the use-ventilated Willies pickup, it felt like there was nothing to stop the wind-inside or out.

"How much further?"

"We're just about there right now." In the dim headlights I could see the edge of the barbed wire fence as we stopped. "O.K. Let's just get over the fence and the pit is out there a little. Be sure to bring your coffee and sandwiches. It could be a while."

The ground wasn't frozen but it was beginning to feel a little more solid than it had earlier in the year. We crunched along through a summer fallow strip watching our breath in the late Fall air, and continued into the middle of a stubble strip. Right there in the stubble Jack leaned over and picked up a chicken wire mesh screen outlined by four two by fours nailed into a rectangle. The chicken wire screen was covered with straw left behind by the combine that had harvested the wheat. First we placed our shotguns, coffee and breakfast in the pit. Then Jack handed me a roll of toilet paper. No kidding.

"What in the hell is this for?"

"Just watch what I do and you do the same."

With that he began to tear off two foot hunks of the tissue and let the ever-present wind blow them away into the stubble field. As they landed, they stuck on the grain stubble standing some 6 to 8 inches high and just waved in the breeze. Jack kept walking in a somewhat circular pattern dispensing his bathroom multi-purpose tissue. I followed his example. He was the teacher, I, the pupil.

"What's the deal?"

"Decoys."

Under the screen we discovered our new home. We stepped down, pulled the screen over us, and settled

in for the first call of the geese rising off Lake Francis
going to the grain fields for breakfast. Jack had dug a
dirt bench and a lower place for our feet. It was actually
comfortable.

"Say, Jack, do you have any three and a half inch number
twos. I'm thinking that a magnum 12 gauge might just
reach on up there where they fly."

"Ya, I do. Here, take a handful."

"Thanks."

I loaded them into the magazine until it was full.
Then pumping one into the chamber, I loaded in one
more shell. Never hurts to be prepared.

Jack's coffee cup was steaming and it smelled
like coffee **should** on a **work** morning. I poured some
from my thermos and we sat there not saying a word and
not feeling the need to break the silence. I guess
sometimes just being there is the important thing. It's
not something that needs explanation. If somebody said,
"God, this is great!", it would spoil the moment.

Since the only sandwich I know how to construct
is the ever popular tuna fish salad sandwich, guess what I
had for breakfast. I like mine with a large dose of dill
pickles cubed so small that you have to ask, "What **is**
that in there?" Also, there's a huge difference between

mayonnaise and Miracle Whip. This may be the first time it has appeared in print. Mayonnaise--no way. Miracle Whip--Oh yeah.

"Shh! Listen!"--Pause--"Did ya hear that?"
"What?"
"They're comin up off the lake."
I couldn't hear a thing. I took another bite of Charley Tuna. Then I heard it. If you have ever been under a flock of geese you'll know what I mean when I say the American Indian's war cry as depicted by Hollywood emulated a flock of geese. Since Valier was a part of what is known as the Central Flyway, it's not uncommon to have flocks of geese completely darken the sky for over half an hour during our part of their migration - either North in the Spring or South in the Fall. With that many geese flying overhead it is sometimes actually difficult to hear what your partner might be saying.
"O.K. Get ready. When they come over they'll be high. They'll spot the paper decoys and I'll hit the call. With any luck they'll circle around lower for a second look. Don't move. Don't even breath. I think they can see the heat of our bodies coming out of the

straw over us, but we'll just have to take our chances on that. If they don't sense anything wrong, they'll make one more pass at the lowest level.   That third time they'll be in good range. That's when we'll throw up the blind and fire away. Remember, pick out an individual goose and give him plenty of lead. He'll be going about 60 or 70 miles an hour and you need to lead him."

"There they are. Over there. Ahh. They're going East. No good."

The cold from the ground was beginning to creep through my pants and jacket. I could stand it, but it was noticeable. I blew hot air through my hands and rubbed them together. A little more coffee from my thermos would take care of the chill.   Besides, I hadn't finished my tuna sandwich.   Somehow it was not shaped like a sandwich any longer. It resembled some sort of white sea cucumber which hadn't ever come of age. It still did smell and taste like tuna. I wonder what it is about tuna salad sandwiches that make them taste so good and makes them at the same time give a person such heartburn. Whatever it is, I know I finally had to quit eating them years ago.

"Hey! Look over there. God, they're right on top of us." Jack blowing on the goose call. They were coming right over the top of us but too high to take. With Jack on the call and the white tissue blowing in the breeze it was as though the geese just couldn't believe their good luck. I envisioned all their long necks bending down and gawking. As they flew over it was too much for them and they turned in a tight descending arc and came in for a second look. Jack's face was beginning to turn a special shade of purple from the honking he was producing. He must have been speaking their language because here they came for a third and final approach.

"O.K. Get ready! --- Now!"

Up pops the screen. Out come the shotguns. Off go the geese. Suddenly I was completely out of shells and could hardly remember firing a single shot. Two geese were going down in the field. The rest were now long gone.

"I got that one over there. Did you get the other one, or did I?"

"I don't have any idea. I just shot all my shells. I think I may have been flock shooting."

The Prize

I had no idea wild geese are loaded with little black crawling creatures. I didn't want to appear stupid, but I also didn't like the little black bugs on the Snow Geese. "What the heck are these little black bugs crawling all over the geese, Jack?"

"Oh, those are just lice. They're on all the geese. When you dunk the goose in boiling water to help with plucking the feathers, they will all be killed. No big deal."

"Here, let's just set these two up out here with the tissue to add to the decoys. That was just the first of many coming in from the lake."

A couple more flights came fairly close that day but none were close enough to decoy in. About an hour after that first flight we decided to abandon the pit in favor of the relative comfort of the pickup. We spent most of the remainder of the morning wandering the back roads of the area in quest of a feeding flock. If we came upon geese feeding in a field, and they took flight, they might fly over us at an acceptable height, and we would be able to pick off one or two.

The Continuing Quest

Soon we noticed the flocks were beginning to head back to Lake Francis. They were done feeding for the morning and were returning to rest. We noticed a group up high a long way off heading back and decided to intercept them in their journey. We drove to the place that looked about right and stopped. We jogged down the road, jumped over the fence, and dashed out in the field. Lying down, we covered ourselves, as best we could, with straw, and awaited the approaching geese. Their riotous conversations were coming directly at us and the volume indicated they were coming in low.

"NOW!"

The Pain

They were directly overhead and in range! Flat on my back, I lifted my trusty Remington to my shoulder and, taking careful aim, allowing for a good lead, touched off my last shot of the morning. My right shoulder was immediately filled with a bright and marvelous pain. Now my shoulder, now my arm, now

my neck, now my head, even my eyes. What the hell?!
Bright lights… Okay, Okay, I'm coming back. Deep
breath. Let it out easy. Another.

A 12 gauge shotgun has an interesting recoil. A
lot of people place a shock absorbing pad on the butt of
the gun to make it a little easier to shoot. I, being of
sound mind, had neglected to do that. I figured if a guy
was going to shoot the thing, he ought to be man enough
to do it the way it came from the manufacturer.   Lying
flat there on the semi-frozen ground, the only place for
the energy from the shotgun to dissipate was my
shoulder. "Hey, you got that one, clean."--pause--
look--"You O.K.?"

Sitting up, "Ya, no problem. Cool. Really neat."

I hadn't even seen the goose go down. Struggling to my
feet and pretending everything was alright, I stumbled
over to my dead, white, lice-ridden prize. The feeling
was beginning to return to my right shoulder and arm
which was a mixed blessing. Cradling my shotgun with
my right arm I leaned down and grabbed my goose by
the neck.

"Well, I don't know about you, but I'm about
ready to head on home. You got four, and I got two. I'm

thinkin' 'at's a pretty good mornin." My entire right side was killing me. I just hoped that Jack would agree.

"Well, we could head up, over North of the lake. There still might be a couple a late flights coming in from there."

"Naw," I rasped. "I'm about done. Let's just head on in."

Show and Tell

At the trailer, (we called it a Mobile Home), it was Show and Tell Time for Betty and Larry Jr. Betty appeared to be interested and Larry Jr. was fascinated with the dead geese. "Are we going to get to keep these two here, Dad?"

"You bet."

The Second Show and Tell

After Jack climbed back in his outfit and took off for home, I continued my Show and Tell Time for Betty by removing my shirt. By that time I had a black and blue bruise that started at the right side of my neck and went down my right arm to the elbow, and a huge bruise on my right side from my armpit, across my chest and back, down to my waist. I was unable to raise my arm above my shoulder.

"I think you better see the doctor."

Of course the doctor was 26 miles away in Conrad. "Nah. I'll be all right. I just hammered myself into the ground with the butt of the gun."

I eased down in my favorite green trailer house high-backed chair and placed my feet on the matching green trailer house ottoman. "Say, Hon. Could I ask you to please get me a couple Excedren?" I asked Larry Jr. to please turn on our 13 inch black and white Zenith. We had two channels. One was a Great Falls station that was rebroadcast for Conrad and the surrounding communities. The other was from a Canadian town up North of us. The Canadian channel was mostly snow with occasional darker images flitting across the screen. I always checked out that channel in hopes that it would be clear. Once in a while we could actually see figures on the tube and hear the dialog. I leaned back to resume a now painful return to my interrupted pre-dawn siesta.

That was the last time I used any kind of

powerful shotgun or rifle for some time.

I learned to direct with my left hand for a time.

I left the geese behind our trailer in a tin bucket, meaning to clean and eat them later. They froze there and were forgotten, covered by a small snow drift for the entire winter. With the spring thaws, I noticed a strange odor emanating from the general area back there and noticed our cat, Smokey, and several other neighborhood cats, and Prince, our Golden Retriever, and Cocoa, our rag-mop dog, spending time back there. Upon investigation, I discovered the rotting, thawing, partly eaten, carcasses of two snow geese. I couldn't help myself. Lice or no lice? Feather by feather I examined a part of one of the geese. No sign of the little black guys. How about that?

Into the garbage… to bad… maybe next fall.

All I could do right then was shake my head and massage my right shoulder.

Mr."O"

Immaculate! That was Ed Olechovski. Neat was not enough. Tidy just didn't cover it. Orderly wasn't sufficient. *"Mr. O."* was style itself and cheerful to a fault. In addition to that, he was punctual--not early--not late--on time. As I remember it, some of the guys in the teachers' lounge set their watches by his morning appearance there.

"Cheerio, and top of the morning to you all. And it is a **fine** morning." That would be Ed's pre-school morning greeting on a Monday after a three-day weekend. Needless to say, he was usually greeted with a profound rebuff, which didn't seem to affect him at all. In those days, it was fashionable to be smoking a cigarette, drinking black coffee, and grousing in preparation for the day. We certainly were not prone to accept Ed's early morning hail with the positive spirit in which it was given.

Ed's teaching assignment was in the area of the Languages; English, French and Drama. His High School plays were always presented to enthusiastic, standing room only audiences. Teaching French gave him a platform to display his gormet cooking skills. In fact this gourmand was well known throughout the county for his unusual requests down at Curry's Grocery —specialty chef items with which no one in Pondera County was acquainted. His teaching style and technique were admired by the students and appreciated by the parents. As a beginning teacher I often wondered what is was like to be his student but would never presume to invade his classroom.

In addition, he was a connoisseur of what he considered fine music. "Bach. Aaaahhh, Bach," He would say while making a fist of his right hand. "Bach is the meat and potatoes of music. Solid, and yet contrapuntal. As Arthur Miller might say, **stolid**, yet with spice."

"Now Mozart, on the other hand. Here we have the Musical Soufflé." With his hands inscribing circles in the air above his head and standing on tiptoe, he could be heard to say, "Careful, we don't wish to make it all fall in upon itself." If he wasn't careful, he might be inscribing those circles on the ceiling, considering his rather long frame.

We are all creatures of habit. We figure out how to make these mindless rituals work for us or against us

in our day to day existence. Ed was no different in this
regard. One workday morning, early, the suave and
debonair Mr. O. appeared at the teachers' work room in
an obvious state of dishevelment. He hadn't shaved, his
hair was uncombed, and his rumpled clothing appeared
to have been too long in the severe Valier wind.

"Hey, Ed. Ya didn't stand too close ta the razor
this morning, did ya? That was from a smirking Joe
Russell, coach and Social Studies teacher.

Raising the flat of his hand to his cheek with a
slight frown of annoyance, Ed rubbed lightly. "Dog-
gone-it, you know what happened. This morning I put
my left sock on before my right and I've had to think
about everything I've done since then."

Ed left, went home, finished his morning
preparations and returned before the beginning bell,
looking completely unperturbed. That was the only time
we were ever permitted to see Mr. O in anything but a
totally groomed state.

Ed was single. I was sure he would prefer to be
responsible solely for himself, rather than have to be
concerned about fitting another person into his
seemingly uncomplicated and well ordered life. He
surprised the entire countryside when he went home to

his beloved South Carolina during the summer school hiatus and returned with a wife, Boo. Of course she was as totally cultured as Ed—anxious to meet and to please all the folks in her new home. You can't imagine her reaction to the winter in Valier. Not only did this fine southern lady experience culture shock. Is there such a thing as weather shock?

It was shortly after returning from summer vacation that   Ed, finding me alone in the hall one day, proposed the following, "Larry, Boo and I would to invite you and Betty and your son over to our home sometime soon for dinner. We could spent a pleasant evening and get to know each other a little better."

"Gee, Ed. I know that both Betty and I would be happy to visit. What night did you have in mind?"

"Actually, I would prefer to be able to do this on a Friday or Saturday night. That way we don't have to think about going to school the next day and we can relax in comfort. What would you say to next Friday? Of course, I know you will need to confer with Betty, right?"

"Tell ya what Ed. Let's just go on ahead and set it up for Friday. I'm sure it'll be okay with Betty. I'll check just to make sure. If we can't do it, I'll let ya know." Betty was thrilled to be invited to Mr. O's home.

As you might expect, Ed's home was neat, clean, and in general a showplace of incredible simplicity and order. The table was set with stoneware of some wonderful vintage. They had provided a salad plate on top of the dinner plate. The coffee cups and saucers were of a stoneware fashion meant to compliment the other dinnerware. Salad forks, regular forks, a knife for general use, a steak knife, a spoon for stirring coffee if needed, a spoon for eating, a variety of glassware including water and wine, adorned the table. In addition, candles cast their soft light on the table and the room. Works of art gave the walls of the living room a reason for standing. On the turntable, Saint Saiens' *Carnival of the Animals* was filling the room.

"Good evening. Please come in. I thought *The Carnival of the Animals* would be appropriate for Larry Jr. How old are you now young man?"

Larry, with big eyes, "I'm five, going on six."

Ed, with a twinkle, "I'm quite sure it is more like five going on thirty. Wouldn't you say folks?"

After a meal, served in courses, (even the Jack Club in Great Falls couldn't compare to that) including tossed salad with a special dressing, green beans, baked potato with sour cream, butter and sprig of parsley, sirloin steak, with a garlic sauce of some kind, a fine red wine that Betty and I both appreciated, peach cobbler for desert accompanied by strong, hot, black coffee, we adjourned to the stuffed chairs and sofas and chatted in the most elegant atmosphere in Valier. In fact, it may have been the most elegant spot in the entire State of Montana.

We would never know what forces combined to get this gentleman giant to move from his beloved homeland to this small Montana town with its unyielding wind, rugged winters, and flat prairie topography. We enjoyed speculating, perhaps a failed love affair? An affair of honor? Maybe a premature mid-life crisis. Whatever the reason, all of Valier admired and respected Ed. We all were proud he had chosen us to share in his life. However, after one Valier winter Ed and Boo returned to Charleston, SC. The Southern Gent and his Southern Belle left many friends and admirers in Valier. They say that no one person's presence will be missed when he is replaced by a new staff member. "If you put your hand in a bucket of water and pull it back out, look at what remains." Not true with Ed. Not only did the school and town miss this tall elegant South Carolinian, but of course the teachers all had to set their watches by the school clock.

Roger

Warren burst into the chorus rehearsal. "Mr. Brasen, Roger is just laying there on the coaches' table all purple and not breathing!"

"What?"

"He's not breathing!"

Roger had not been feeling well, and had asked permission to leave the chorus rehearsal to rest in the coaches room just across the hall. He played Tuba in band, sang lead Tenor in chorus, and was a leader on the Championship Football Team. He had proven himself to be a reliable, dependable young man. Knowing I could trust him, I had allowed him to go by himself to the P.E. office area to rest. After ten minutes or so, I sent Warren , another student, to the dressing room, to check on Roger.

To Warren, "Quick, get Mr. Van Gordon." Then to all the others in the room, "You all stay in your places."

I don't remember the few steps it took to get across the hall. Roger was lying on his back, on the narrow steel wrapping table, three feet above the tiled

[

floor. His swollen face was the color of blueberry pie. "Roger, Roger," I screamed, running to him. His chest had expanded to nearly half again it's normal size and as I pushed down on it with all my force, I realized he was not going to exhale.

His arm, which had been hanging down from the table, flew up and across his chest with such force, he rolled to his left off the table, falling the three feet onto the tile. I caught his head and cushioned it from hitting the floor.

The door flew open and the Principal, Charles Van Gordon, dashed in. He immediately began applying mouth to mouth resuscitation. Gasp. "Call the ambulance!" Gasp. Blow. "He's not letting any air out."

By this time the room had filled with kids and teachers from all over the school. "Larry, get everyone out of here, and keep them out."

"Back to your rooms, everyone, back to your rooms."

As I herded my students back onto the stage, where we rehearsed, we heard the ambulance siren. We could see the lights flashing as it backed up to the rear door closest to the coaches office. Then it was gone.

[

Roger was on the twenty-six mile trip to Conrad, the nearest hospital and medical staff.

Bonnie, Roger's girl friend, was audibly sobbing in the arms of a couple of her best girl friends. We waited in stunned silence for a report on Roger's progress from Mr. Milne.

Time isn't a constant. It expands and contracts according to urgency-*time flies when you're having fun*-time wasn't going anywhere right then. It had become a dark shroud, numbing the minds and stopping the tongues of even the brightest in the room.

"Good morning to the entire High School. This is Mr. Milne speaking to you. I know everyone is concerned about Roger. As you know, he is being taken by ambulance to the hospital in Conrad. We have been in radio contact with the emergency people in the ambulance and the news is that Roger is breathing with the assistance of the machinery aboard. They are nearing the hospital and we should have additional news soon. In the meantime, might I suggest that you all attempt to return to normal activities.   I'll be updating you as soon as we hear anything new." The metallic click disconnecting the intercom, closed the lid on that room.

The period ended with the buzzer. The students

[

filed out of the room in silence. Kids walked with unseeing eyes through the halls. I made my way to the teacher's work room. Joe and Ed were already there. Jack popped his head in.

"Anybody hear anything?"

Bruce Milne came in with a smile that split his face in two. "He's okay." He was laughing, crying, and shaking his head. "He's okay. He hyperventilated. That's all. He'll be back in school this afternoon."

The news swept through the school, lifting spirits, returning everything to near normal. In fact, Bonnie and a couple of other of Roger's friends met in the music area during lunch and started thinking about having a little party for Roger's return.

From that day forward, Roger carried a little paper sack folded in his hip pocket. Whenever he started to get that uncomfortable feeling, a prolog to hyperventilating, he simply opened the sack, held it to his mouth, and breathed in and out until he returned to normal.

It kind of gives a whole new meaning to "Brown Bagging It".

ICE FISHING

The year was 1967. Betty and I were teaching at Valier Public Schools while Larry Jr. attended Kindergarten there. It was following another rather dismal showing on the hardwood that my friend Jack, the Basketball Coach, asked, "Larry, you ever been ice fishing?"

I had heard of ice fishing but I had to admit the opportunity had never presented itself. "No, I never have,"
I replied. "But from what I've heard about it, I'm sure I'd like it."

"Well, the ice is pretty thick on Lake Francis, and I hear they've been takin' 'bows and Pike. Jya like to give it a go?"

"You betcha. When?"

"Ya know, I got an ice house. Nice. Four by Eight. It could use a little stove. I could weld one together in shop. I could save the hardwood scraps from the projects and saw them into inch square pieces to burn. They'd burn hot."

By Monday after basketball practice, Jack had

figured out the pieces of the stove he needed to weld together. While I watched through dark glasses or looked away, Jack welded together a stove that was about eighteen inches by eighteen inches by six inches, with a little door in front for allowing additional fuel. On the top of the stove He had cut and then welded a stovepipe fitting. He cut a hole in the roof of the ice house that allowed the 3 inch stove pipe to exit the six foot tall roof. He welded four small feet onto the little stove so it could sit up, off the floor. We were definitely ready!

"Okay. Let's plan on Sunday morning. I'll pick you up at about Five O'clock. That'll give us plenty of time to do everything we need to do. Before we quit tonight, let's get the icehouse loaded into the back of the pickup."

I actually woke up before the alarm. I had everything ready, including the canned corn and the canned shrimp. My thermos filled with coffee and the trusty tuna fish sandwiches with dill pickles were complete and waiting. I also had a little bit of butter, a little bit of honey, and a liberal supply of rum, purchased from Marie Devini down at the local State Liquor Store. The pole, tackle box, and lunch were waiting on the counter next to the door. With Jack's blinking of the Willies lights, we were off.

Lake Francis is only a few moments from town. The dam and the resulting lake were built to supply a vast irrigation project out on that flat country envisioned by some unknown engineer. The resulting lake provided the residents and visitors alike with a wonderful recreational facility.

Jack drove up on the dyke in the dark pre-dawn, and West until he was able to get his pickup down to the shore of the lake. Without even pausing, he gave it the gas and went on out on the frozen lake. "Hey, what the hell ya doin'?

"Just drivin' on out."

"What in the hell're we on?"

"Ice," was Jack's reply.

"How deep?"

"An inch'll hold up a locomotive."

At that point Jack turned his pickup in a 180. Applying his brakes, we came to a stop. "Okay, let's get this baby out of the box."

Opening the door of the pickup against the wind, I was immediately reminded why I wore my parka. The temperature was well below zero and the wind was sneaking right up my right coat sleeve. Snow didn't accumulate on the frozen lake because of the constant barrage of the Westerlies.

The preacher of one of the churches, I don't remember which, went missing late one night. He was last seen pitching a tent he was experimenting with as an ice-fishing house. When he didn't return home on this fateful night, a search party was convened. His car was discovered not far from the Lighthouse Bar/café on the Dike. By nine o'clock that night his tent was found in a barbed wire fence on the East side of the lake. That would place the tent only a few blocks West of the town. At about ten o'clock that night, he walked in his front door a bit bedraggled but really none the worse for wear. He explained that the wind got hold of his tent and became a sail from which he refused to detach himself. It blew him all the way from the Lighthouse Café/Bar across the ice covered lake to the East end where he walked home. He said he was sorry for causing the trouble for everyone but I think he was really sorry when it all came out in the town's weekly mimeographed newsletter later in the week.

I hunched up my shoulders and squinted through my thirty M.P.H. breeze eyes. Jack had grabbed hold of the rope attached to each of the runners on the bottom of the ice house. With one big pull, about a third of it emerged beyond the pickup box. I grabbed one side and with Jack on the other we lifted and coaxed the front end of the ice house out and down on to the ice. Moving to the back, we eased it out of the pickup and forward, clearing the tailgate, and down to the ice.

Jack got back in the pickup, started it up, and drove over to the shore, parking it safely away from the lake. There were stories about guys that parked on the ice in the winter and went fishing. If it happened too late in the winter there was a chance their outfit would not be seen again.

Grabbing the rope, we pulled our new temporary home out onto the ice where Jack was sure there would be a healthy supply of the under-ice denizens. We positioned the ice house strategically and Jack opened the door. Inside he had two hinged one foot square ice hole trap doors, in the floor, on opposite corners of the four by eight floor plan. I watched with interest as, opening the doors, he scratched an X in the ice, marking each door.

We then moved the house forward on its runners exposing both marks. Jack then went to work with an ice auger, an eight inch wide iron corkscrew, ending with a crossbar of one inch metal, about six feet above the ice. Screwing the auger into the ice we created a hole eight inches wide. At about 18 to 24 inches we struck water. Pulling the auger out and back in several times we cleared most of the ice particles from the hole. After doing the same for the second mark, we moved the ice house back over the holes.

We entered the ice house. Outside, the cold and the ever-present wind, was cutting new wrinkles on even old faces. Closing the door, the interior was a little warmer, and we felt no air movement. Jack turned on a flashlight.

"Well, let's clear our ice holes." Jack grabbed a small strainer meant for tea I think, and proceeded to clear the remaining small ice flotsam and fresh water shrimp from his ice hole. Baiting his hook with an earthworm, he lowered his line down in the hole.

I did the same and looked down in the ice hole with the aid of the flashlight. I was unable to see much down there and turning I noticed that Jack was starting a fire in the new stove. Placing some newspaper and kindling in the stove he applied a match. As the flames started to eat the smaller sacrificial fire starters, Jack slipped in some of the one inch cubes supplied by the leftovers from the shop projects. The fire caught, and already we could feel the air inside the ice house beginning to warm.

I settled back, unzipped my coat, removed my hood, poured some coffee from my thermos, and warmed my ever-chilled hands above the stove. Jack did the same and at that point I noticed a soft glow beginning to emanate from my ice hole. As the sun rose, it illuminated the water under the ice. Looking down, I was able to identify my bait, the lake bottom, plants, and, "Jack, there's a great big Rainbow in my hole," I whispered.

"I know. He was just over here."

He nosed my bait. I stopped breathing. I jigged the line a little. He moved beyond my sight. Wait… seconds jogged by. I started to pull my line in to readjust the bait on the hook when from under my line the trout was coming up for the bait. All I could see was mouth. Closing on the hook, he turned and with a powerful thrust of his tail, began to disappear from my field of vision. I pulled up on the line, which I was holding in my bare hand, encountering a sudden jolt. "I got him!"

"Pull 'im right on up out of the hole!" Jack yelled.

Suddenly I had a healthy 2 pound Rainbow Trout flopping in my lap, on the hot stove, on Jack, on the floor, "Open the door and throw him out on the ice."

As I opened the door, the fish spit the hook out of his mouth and flipped right out on the ice. "Should I knock him on the head?"

"Naa. He'll freeze out there. He's not goin anywhere," Jack said. "Well, how jya like it?"

My heart was attempting to return to it's pre-hundred-yard-dash rate, but since my breathing was returning to near normal, I was able to reply, "That is fantastic!"

For the next hour or so we continued to fish at that spot. Several times we had Pike or Trout in our holes. Jack landed one or two trout and I missed a couple. About the only thing either of us found it necessary to say was, "I got one in." The ice hole was a window on a natural aquarium. While it afforded a somewhat limited view, I still found it fascinating.

Getting lulled into a pattern of "Got one in" and waiting, I was suddenly startled by what I thought was a gun shot followed by a horrible groaning. Then I realized the noise was coming from the ice. "What the hell!" I opened the door, ready to get off the ice.

"Hey, whoa," Jack said.

"What was that?" I figured the ice was breaking up and we were goners.

"That's jest the ice talkin' to us. Happens all the time. It is always cracking and groaning like that. We're on a couple feet of ice out here. Nothin' to worry about.

When the action slowed, Jack opened a can of corn and spilled some of it's contents into the hole. I did the same. At first the juice from the corn blurred the scene somewhat. Then, as it dissipated, I was able to see the corn slowly drifting to the bottom. Some of it disappeared from view under the plant growth. Some of it actually came to rest on the plants and remained in sight.

Waiting for a while longer to see if the "salting" of the hole brought any new reed dwellers out to play, we decided to move to another spot. We became the "Nomads of Lake Francis Ice Fishermen".

At one point, we heard a guy yelling and swearing outside. As I went to open the door, he was pounding on it and continuing to yell. Shielding my eyes from the much brighter light outside, the first thing I noticed was bright red blood on the ice and more blood pouring from the man's hand.

"What the hell happened?"

"I landed a Pike and he bit down on my hand between my thumb and finger. I jerked back and he cut me bad. Ya got anything could help?"

Jack, nodding his head up and down in understanding, said, "I got a couple Band Aids in my jockey box over in the truck back there."

"Maybe pack it with snow and get to town," I said.

"God damn! Where's the nearest doctor?"

"Over to Conrad, right?" I said, looking at Jack for agreement.

As he turned and started away, I noticed he was holding his arm up over his head. Good move, I thought. Keep the hand above his heart.

We didn't get his name or anything. Jack said, "If you ever get bit by a pike like that, don't jerk away. They got razors for teeth. Calmly open its mouth and take it off your hand." Since we didn't read or hear about anyone dying of pike bite during the next week we assumed he must have made it okay.

After lunch, Jack dug out an old, empty, three pound Folgers Coffee can. The water he scooped from the ice hole, contained some fresh water shrimp, which were nearly transparent creatures, less than an inch long, on which the fish thrive. He set it on the stove to heat. Once boiling, using our coffee cups, we put in some butter, some honey, some rum, and poured in the bubbling water. The result was a relaxing and tasty brew.

Waking up a little later, over my ice hole, I could feel the chill in the air. "Hey, I think I nodded off there for a minute."

Stirring, Jack said, "Ya. Maybe we better build the fire back up."

"What time is it, anyway? God, is it two o'clock already?"

"Hey, ya know, I think we better go on ahead and load on up," Jack said.

We picked up several frozen trout and one 16 inch pike I had managed to land. Jack went over and brought the pickup out to the ice house. Loading the ice house back into the pickup box, we left the ice and once again were on the dike, headed toward the Lighthouse Bar/café. We decided we would go directly home, electing not to stop in for a beer, visiting, and some "bumper pool", in the bar.

At home, I brought two or three trout and one pike inside to clean. Since the fish were frozen solid, they had to thaw before cleaning, so we ran the kitchen sink full of water and placed the fish there to soften enough so the knife could do its work.

Larry Jr. was extremely interested in the fish. It was a bigger catch than I had ever brought home. Not a "Poplar North Fork Sucker" in the bunch. All of them edible. He reached his hand up to feel the fish in the water when the pike flipped his tail, nearly jumping out of the water onto the kitchen floor.

"He's alive! My god! He's alive! How can that be? He's alive!"

Jumping up and down, "Let's put him in the tub, Dad." Larry Jr. said.

"Quick. Run some water in the bath tub. I'll get my net."

Soon we had Mr. Pike swimming in our tub. The predator was alive and stalking any moving thing. "Stay back away from the tub, Larry. That fish can really bite you."

There we were, my son and I, fascinated by the trophy swimming in our tub.

My mind flashed back to my dad, standing knee deep in the North Fork of the Poplar, and me frozen mid-catch.

I put my hand on my son's shoulder and stood there with him in silence.

Thanks, Dad.

Maybe That Wasn't So Clever After All

It is Big Sky Country. Not all of Montana has the proverbial Big Sky. Betty and I and our son Larry, spent 3 years in Eureka, Montana. We moved there after teaching 2 years in Valier, and after having spent our lives in Eastern and Central Montana, which is mostly treeless flat land and rolling hills. Eureka was a small logging town in the Rocky Mountains of Northwestern Montana. It was nestled amid mountains in all directions. In fact, with the winter burning of slash piles left during the summer logging activities, the skies would be clouded with smoke all winter. The sun, when it did make it's appearance, was identified as an UFO. That was definitely not *Big Sky* Country.

Arriving out of the West, on Highway US 2, under Glacier Park, out onto the American Great Plains, the land of the Maria and the Missouri opened before us, as our very spirits responded, opening to the potential life held for us. The Big Sky Country will do that for a person.

February in Valier caught most of us still hunkered down in our houses, spending as little time outdoors as possible. I guess that in 1965-66 the great

Snowmobile Virus had not yet gathered its present momentum, infecting so many Montanans. Of course, I had become addicted to ice fishing. Jack Dunlap and I had fished on a lot of great lakes that winter, including the famous Mission Lake, which had 2 inch long fresh water shrimp to feed the Brook Trout population. One of the record trout ever caught in a lake had come from that body of water. That year, we were catching Brookies averaging two pounds.

We took home our limits and filleted them. We then rolled them in a special beer batter of Jack's concocting. Karen rounded up a large cast iron fry pan and filled it with some kind of grease, a combination of Crisco and Butter, I think, and then submerged the coated pink Brook trout fillets in the roiling liquid.

We had spent some time over in the Flathead Lake area, earlier in the fall. The West shore of Flathead Lake was filled with Cherry Orchards in those years. The owners offered to sell Cherries at roadside stands, by the little wooden crate, paper sack, or entire flats. Another option was the infamous U-Pick. That was the option we chose. Larry and Betty and I went into the orchard and ate/picked our way through as many trees as possible. It was a good thing they didn't weigh us before and after. The amount we ate was significant. After paying for the cherries we picked, we eventually made cherry preserves and my home made cherry wine. The house would be filled with the smell of yeast working on the cherries smashed in the cheese cloth covered fifteen gallon stone crock. Having completed the wine making, I bottled the finished product in quart beer bottles and capped them with a home bottle capper.

I brought my souvenir wine skin filled with the cherry wine along to go with the fried fish. The more we ate the better the wine tasted and the more we drank the better the fish tasted. With school coming up the following day, we left the Dunlap's fairly early that Sunday. We hadn't been home long when both Betty and I were attacked by a dreadful case of gastro-intestinal explosiveness. The combination of the deep fried fish, beer batter, and cherry wine made life interesting for the remainder of the evening and into the next morning.

I looked closely at Jack the following morning in the teachers work room before school. I couldn't tell if the Dunlaps had experienced any adverse reactions from our feast or not. That was the code of Montana guys. If you partook in excess the night before, you got up and went to work the following day as though everything

was just fine. If for some reason you were unable pay
the fiddler the morning after, you had no right dancing
the dance the night before.

It was at that fish fry that I believe it was Karen
that suggested, "Next time you guys go ice fishin', I
think Betty and I ought to go along with ya'."

"I think you're absolutely right," I said.

Jack replied, "What do you say we hit Lake
Francis next week end?"

With that, the next weekend was set in stone. We
would be up early, out on the dike and onto the lake with
the pickup and ice house. Karen and Betty would park
over by the Lighthouse Bar/cafe, and trek out to the ice
house after Jack and I got it all set up.

We had fished the lake enough to have a good
idea of where the best chances of catching Rainbows
would be, although predicting fish in the lake was
playing by ear at best. When the temperature was below
zero and the wind swept the ice at 30 miles an hour, it
was fingertips, toes, cheeks, and nose. Betty and Karen
were bundled against the weather. Even at that, their
faces were pink with the exertion of walking in that
temperature. They had slipped and fallen on the ice,
fighting the wind, and the air was filled with their

laughter as they arrived at the ice house.

Inside, as soon as the door was closed, and their eyes grew accustomed to the dark, they were drawn to the eerie light emanating from the ice holes. "Wow, look at that. Hey, you can see right down into the water. It's just like an aquarium. Karen, can you see down there?"

We baited the hooks and lowered them into the holes, surrendering the lines to the gals. Betty was fishing in the hole closest to the door with me, and Karen was at the back with Jack.

"Fish in!" It was Karen.

"Easy," Jack. "Leave it alone. Wait. Wait. Okay. Jig it a little."

"He's goin' over your way."

"He's in over here. Pull it up slow and easy. He might go for it." Wait--Wait-- "He's gone."

"Hey, Betty, let's trade. I'd like to see how it looks over there."

"Okay."

Karen was now in my spot. "Fish in! He took it! He took it!"

"Pull 'im in! Pull, pull."

"Oh, I got 'im. What now?"

"Get 'im up outta the hole."

"He's off!"

The Rainbow Trout had been all the way out of the hole when he threw the hook and slid back into the icy domain from which he had come. Without thinking, my hand snaked down the side of the hole, the back of my hand moving against the ice. At shoulder length I spread my fingers across the bottom of the hole and brought my hand up with the speed of light. Amid the ice water, ice crystals, and hook, line, and sinker, was a wonderful two pound trout which landed, flapping in Karen's lap. Of course, laughing, screaming, and in general sounding as if we were being accosted by <u>the Mutant Gator Fish of the lake</u>, we eventually gained control of the fish and pitched it out on the ice to freeze. Our first prize of the day.

Those were the only fish in our holes. After some time, we decided to move the ice house. When Jack and I suggested we move, the girls were very agreeable. In fact, it became apparent that they had ulterior motives.

Betty said, "Well, as long as we're moving and not coming back to this spot, would you guys mind if we girls had a private moment?"

Jack had installed a hook and screw eye on the

outside of the ice house door, to lock it in transport. Once on the ice, without even consulting with each other, we promptly slid the hook into the screw eye. Picking up the rope that formed the triangle to the runners on the ice house, we waited. Okay, the belts are probably undone. Okay, the trousers are probably coming down. Okay, let's go.

Pulling with all our strength, we took that ice house and it's occupants on the wildest ride of their lives. Round and round, let's stop. Oh no, let's go again. Screaming from the interior. When stopped, the door was about to be pounded down. Move again.

On the inside, of course there was nothing to hold onto. Not only was it dark, but the stove was hot. Later, Betty told me that the experience was not nearly as funny as it was truly terrifying. Outside, the girls screams seemed so funny to us that it just inspired us to continue the torture, even though we knew when we stopped we would need to provide a reason for our actions.

As Karen and Betty emerged from the door, ashen faced, we knew we were in trouble. Since I am telling the story, I am going to choose to omit the ensuing conversation including the choices Jack and I

might have to make if we ever did anything like that
again. Actually, when we saw how frightened they were,
we were sorry for what we had done. Sometimes I think
a simple apology followed by silence may be the best
solution.

Betty's turn to catch was to come. In fact, when
the score was totaled, the gals out fished the guys that
day. When we wrapped it all up and had the ice house
loaded on the pickup, we stopped in at the Lighthouse
for pizza and beer. Actually, as I remember it, the girls
had coffee and Seven Up, and Jack and I had the beer.
Several other fishermen stopped in on their way home.
Some other townspeople popped in for pizza and beer
and bumper pool. A guitar was produced from
somewhere, and with me playing and leading the
impromptu group, we sang Kingston Trio and Harry
Bellefonte type folk songs and enjoyed each other's
company.

Later that night, just before sleep overtook us,
with Larry asleep in his bed, not having any idea what
prompted my statement, I said, "Ya know, Hon.
Sometimes don't ya just kind of feel like anything ya
want to do or become is somehow just right out there--
just in reach?" "Yah, Cool, Night Hon."

Mama Bear

November 16, 2011 by Betty Brasen

In July of 1967 our son, Larry Jr., was four and a half years old. He was to be an only child, I knew, so I was careful about letting him cross streets alone, play with stray dogs and cats, or play with other children. My friend Karen described my behavior as "over-protective".

With reckless abandon, Jack and Karen Dunlap's son, Johnny, jumped off a garage, dislocating his shoulder; jumped off the bed, twisting his ankle; and ran into a closed door, blacking his eye. The boys were great friends, with Johnny extending the boundaries of their escapades and Larry limiting them.

Our families spent recreation time together. That summer we planned a week-long vacation to Glacier Park, making Lake McDonald Camp Ground our base of operations. Arriving at the camp ground by early evening left plenty of daylight to set up camp, cook supper, and relax before bedtime. My husband, Larry, brought his guitar for the campfire sing-a-long.

Twinkling stars covered the inky sky. Pines-warm from the heat of the day-scented the cooling air with their woodsy fragrance. Waves, lapping the shores of Lake McDonald beat a sleepy rhythm to our singing, laughing and visiting, as we sat comfortably around the campfire on our camp stools and lawn chairs.

The kids, tired from a long day, were ready to crawl into their sleeping bags. Johnny, who had already been up the path to the bathroom and back, jumped into bed with his usual enthusiasm. His sister, Kathy, had gone with her mother earlier and she was snuggled down – her blond hair sweeping her cheeks, her blue eyes already closed in slumber. That left Larry Jr., still needing to trudge up the path before he went to bed. I said I'd go with him, but his dad said he could go by himself. After all Johnny hadn't had any trouble, the bathroom was only about fifty feet away down a straight path so we could watch him all the way.

Off he trotted in his flannel P.J.s, red-plaid flannel bathrobe, and tennis shoes. He was so cute! – determined to perform this errand without Mom's help. I watched as the darkness nearly swallowed his form as he vanished behind the outhouse door—unaware there were two exits to the facility.

In camp, we settled down to visiting while we waited for Larry to return.

But he didn't!

Beginning to get worried, I asked his dad to check on him. He finished the song, put down the guitar, and ambled up the path. He walked in the door calling for Larry. Almost instantly he dashed out the door He yelled, "He's not here! Did I miss him on the path?" Panicked, I ran to where Larry was standing We started calling No answer!

I'd never been an aggressive sort of person, but I certainly changed my tune. Jack, Karen's husband, Larry, and I started searching for my boy.Karen stayed in camp with Johnny and Kathy. Johnny wanted to help look for Larry, Jr., but one lost child was enough. Frantically, we went from camp to camp asking if anyone had seen a little boy in pajamas, plaid bathrobe and tennis shoes wandering around People left their camps to help us look for our son. We came to a group of good ol' boys on a fishing trip. They seemed to think our lost child story was a joke. One of them, a tall, heavy guy made a comment about letting the bears find him. That was the last straw! I went over to the big gorilla, grabbed him by the arm, and jerked him out to the road. Yelling at him, "How would you feel if your four year old boy was lost?" Giving him a shove, I yelled, "Now, get out there and start looking!" The fellow and his friends must have seen me as a real threat to their personal happiness because they left the camp calling, "Hey, Larry Jr.!"

Down the road I went, checking with everyone, calling for him! Then out of darkness, came his sweet little voice, "Hi, Mom! There he was! A lady was holding him. She set him on the ground. He ran over and gave me a huge hug.

We thanked the lady profusely for finding our son. She said, "He was sitting on the cement step when I came out of the bathroom. I asked him why he was sitting there. He told me he was lost, so he sat down knowing his mom and dad would find him if he stayed in one place. I offered to help him find you, but he didn't want to leave. I finally convinced him that it was ok, and we were just leaving to look for you."

We went back to camp the way we had come, telling everyone along the way we had found our son. Even the boys at the end of the loop, who were somewhat embarrassed by their previous behavior, were pleased to see that we had found him.

When we got back to camp, we took Larry over to the bathroom to see how he had managed to miss the path back to the camp so it wouldn't happen again. He showed us the path he had followed to reach the bathrooms on the other side of the campgrounds, where he had decided to wait.

Although this experience was terrifying for me, it was not for our son. He had been confident that his mom and dad would find him if he just stayed in one place.

As I tucked Larry Jr. into his sleeping bag and kissed his precious, trusting face, I decided there was nothing wrong with being a little "overprotective".

Roberts, Montana

A fantastic teaching experience!

Roberts All School Centennial

Background:

After retiring from teaching in 1979 at the age of thirty nine, I spent ten years building our AMWAY business. Spending a monstrous amount of time on the road, helping my distributors in any way I could, I became a little disillusioned with the business in general. I started thinking of what it had been like to teach music in the public educational systems in Montana and the United States Virgin Islands. As in the Amway business, I touched a lot of lives in a positive way in the music teaching business. That had been true of students and adults alike. It was into this shifting attitude that I received a call from my friend, Ron Marshall, the Superintendent of the public schools in Roberts, Montana.

Our conversation:

Ron: Larry, I know that you are busy building the Amway business, but I decided to give you a call anyway. Our present music instructor is leaving at the end of this school year and we will have a vacancy for a full time music man here for next year. Have you ever thought about going back into education? Your positive attitude that you've learned building your Amway business would be just what these kids and this community needs.

Me: Wow, Ron. I'm amazed you would think of me. I have on occasion thought about the times I've had building music programs in the past. But I don't think I'm really your man for this job. Besides, I've let my certification lapse.

Ron: Well, let me tell you that as far as your certification goes, I can get that taken care of in one phone call. Tell you what! Why don't you come over this Wednesday, and see the kids, we can chat, and I'll buy you one of the best school lunches money can buy.

Me: How can I turn that down. What time should I get there?

That was the beginning of five of the best years of teaching I ever spent. When you put together an incredible staff, incredible families, incredible kids, incredible administration, and incredible school board what do you expect? Here is a short description of what happened that next Wednesday.

The Interview:

I drove up to the school, ten miles on a dirt road from where I lived at the time in Bridger, Montana. Parked the car, got out, walked up to the front door and walked inside. Ron's office was to my right behind the office desk. Donna, the secretary, asked if she could help. I said I was there to chat a little with my friend Ron. By this time, Ron was up out of his chair and out into the outer office shaking hands and introducing me to Donna Tande, the secretary. He invited me in to his office and we got comfortable chatting about old times in the Amway business. (He had been one of our distributors at one time) About that time the outside door opened and who should appear at the front desk but a farmer/rancher dressed in his work clothes who came right past the front desk and into the office. Ron said, "Larry, let me introduce you to the chairman of the school board here, Mr. Joe Niemi." The three of us sat and visited a while and then Mr. Niemi excused himself saying, "I've got to be going. Awful nice to meet you Larry and I hope we can expect to see a lot more of you starting next school year."

The Band Class:

Ron said, "The Band Class is about to start up. Let's go in and watch them for a while. I think you'll like what you see."

Band class was held in the cafeteria right next to the office. We had heard them warming up and when they started playing we stepped into the area. I was immediately struck by the fresh scrubbed, country look of all the kids. No purple hair and no visible tattoos. There was a balanced instrumentation, including a Tuba, which a lot of small schools had trouble getting anyone to play. The director recognized me from the many school bands I had directed in the past and offered me the baton. While I wasn't really ready to lead a group after such a hiatus, I jumped at the chance. I loved it!!!

We watched the whole rehearsal and at the end of it with five minutes left in the period, the director stopped and said, "Okay, everybody. Time to pack it up. You know the routine!" The students put their instruments away followed by their stands and then the chairs. Then without a word the boys grabbed hold of the folded cafeteria tables that were stacked against the wall and set them up for lunch. They all lined up and the bell rang dismissing them from class. I was favorably impressed!

The Lunch:

Now it was time for lunch. The ladies, Bev Alt and Gladys Weimer, in the lunch room had been working all morning on the food preparation. We went to the head of the line and were served roast beef, mashed potatoes and gravy, a little mixed carrots and peas, apple crisp and corn bread and coffee. I thought the aroma had been wonderful when we were at the band practice. I get hungry even today just telling about it. Great Chow!

The Question:

After lunch we adjourned back to the office. Ron said, "Well, Larry, what do you think? To which I replied, "Ron. I'm really impressed. I like the looks of the overall operation. I know I'd be proud to be a part of it. It would mean kind of making our Amway business a second class citizen in our lives. I'd need to have a little talk with Betty about the pros and cons. What do you say to me letting you know by Friday morning?" And so we parted company.

The Town:

Roberts is a small community a few miles North of Red Lodge on the highway to Joliet, Rock Vale, Laurel and eventually Billings. When I say "small" I mean as I remember it there were roughly one hundred forty kids in the school including Elementary and High School. That averages out to about ten students per class. Certainly not a large number of students but what an opportunity to get to know the families including extended family members. There were a few homes in town but most of the students lived on farms surrounding the town. The town had a Fire Department, one Cafe, two or three Bars, a Post Office, a couple businesses supplying various goods to farmers and ranchers and builders, a Gas station...in short it was a small Montana town like so many others. And yet it seemed to have an air of something just different enough to pique the curiosity.

The Talk:

Betty and I had a talk that evening. It had been quite a time since we had sponsored anyone new. Working down-line in multi-level marketing is enjoyable but the real action is in personally sponsoring. We were at a point in our business where we could continue to supply our down-line distributors and our personal customers without me being full time in the business. This might be the perfect time to take a sabbatical and get back into teaching. We decided to take the new step in our lives and I would go back into education. Once we made that decision, I was excited out of my mind about the new challenges that lay ahead.

Interlude:

At this point I am skipping ahead to November of 1989. I started teaching at Roberts in late August and had been teaching all the Music Classes in the Grade School including Beginning and Second year Band and High School Band and Chorus plus a special class of Junior High Art Appreciation and a Photo Journalism type class which published a weekly "The Week That Was" picture paper.

The Idea:

This was the Montana Centennial year. I got to thinking about how we could put together a program that described the history of Montana. It could start with Lewis and Clark and their Corps of Discovery, then bring in the fur trappers and the Indians and then the Black Robes(Catholic Priests), followed by gold seekers, the Railroaders, don't forget the Cavalry, the ranchers and farmers. We couldn't tell the history of the state without mentioning bad guys and sheriffs. As the idea took hold in my brain, I started getting source material so I could sequence the entry of each era correctly. Of course some overlapping actually happened but we could ignore that for our little "History".

As the writing started to take shape, it occurred to me that a member of the "cast" would step to a microphone and narrate the story from memory. With each vignette there would be the appropriate music sung and played by soloists and the chorus and band and all the participants. For the finale we could introduce it as at long last all the different people that made Montana a state came together as we ended the play all singing and playing the state song, "Montana". And as it all began to materialize, I took the script and the idea with a rough draft of the costuming and set pieces we would use to Mr. Marshall, the Superintendent. He said, "Larry, I love the whole idea. One of the best educational concepts to come our way in years. We combine History, Public Speaking, Music with the band and chorus, Acting… I want to encourage you to put a lot of effort into this project."

The Plan:

It wasn't long before all the Elementary Teachers were preparing their classes for the big event. The High School/Jr. High band and chorus were ready with their pieces and since there were only a few students in the school that I didn't teach Mr. Marshall and I invited them to participate along with all the teachers in the school to take part. Mr. Marshall was so excited about the program that he called the schools at Joliet, Mt. And Bridger, Mt. And arranged for us to take an entire day with all the school and go on a field trip to those two schools and perform it for them.

You know, a lot of people might be tempted to look down on a school the size of Roberts. If they do, they just don't understand to power of positive thought- the ability to take what you have in hand and create something that had never existed and probably wouldn't ever again. Don't you wonder sometimes what they use their brains for?

The Performance:

The Kindergarten kids were the cows for the First/Second Grade Ranchers and Farmers. All the classes were assigned/chose what segment of the Founders of Montana they represented. They all wore costumes made by the parents for the presentation. Lewis and Clark, Indians with feathers, Fur trappers, Black Robes, Cowboys, Railroaders, Gold seekers complete with pans, Cavalry with their sabers, Farmers and Ranchers (Husband and Wife), Road Agents and Sheriff Posses, and we can't leave out the Politicians all met on the Gym Floor on the BIG NIGHT!

The gym was packed and anticipation was in the air. We made it through the entire program with hardly a single mess up. (A few of the Kindergarten Kows got lost from the herd and had to be rounded up to the amusement of the audience.) And then we came to the climactic ending that introduced the State Song "Montana".

The Finale:

The President of the Student Council stood to the microphone and spoke, "Ladies and Gentlemen, Friends, Guests, and some friends I see from other schools. It is from the very beginning of the state that so many people of so very different backgrounds and belief systems have had to fight each other, care for each other, look out for themselves while leaving their neighbor untrampled, help the rancher raise his barn one day and be in a fight over water rights the next, establish a business in hopes of making a fortune only to wind up giving the miner a stake for a share of nothing,--All these dreams and all this toil is brought together today. We, working together, have hammered out a new state. We come together here and now and invite all in hearing range to join us in singing the Anthem of this Brand New State, "MONTANA"!!!

<u>*Epilogue:*</u>

The following day we loaded up the buses, extra pickups, packed kids and lunches, props, chaperons, teachers—The entire school—and went on the road first to the gym in Joliet where the audience was seated in the bleachers on the second floor. We stopped at Rockvale for a picnic lunch provided by the Bev and Gladys and the school board. Then on to Bridger where we performed in their gym in the afternoon. Then even the most exuberant of the kids had used all the adrenaline they had left. It was a quiet ride on the back road across to Roberts and home.

Roberts all-school Centennial Musical Extravaganza. Here being presented at the Joliet School Auditorium on November 14, 1989.

Preparing To Teach Music At Roberts

Getting Ready:

I had agreed to teach Music for the Roberts, Montana School System for the year 1989-90. One of the first things I had to do was get my certification in order. In chatting with my new boss, Ron Marshall, I discovered that one of the first things I had to do was take some kind of Teacher Test. I had never taken one that was a National Exam so I was a little nervous. Since it was the spring of the year, I had a little time to get my teacher stuff together. I had until early Fall to go.

Checking with the Education Department at Eastern Montana College I found that the test was given about 3 weeks from that date, in the Ed Building on a Saturday morning and afternoon. Yep, that's right! Morning and afternoon! It was a four part test. We were to take the first two sections in the morning and the other in the afternoon.

While at the college, I dropped by the Bookstore. I told the lady behind the counter that I was prepping to take the National Teaching Test. "Is there any kind of material I can buy to help get me ready for it? It's coming up in a short time."

She said, "You bet!!! We have books to prepare you for that exact test. Now, it won't be exactly the current test, but the questions and examples come from actual previous tests that have already been given. I don't think you can go wrong by studying out of this booklet." We had been walking toward the back part of the store and she stopped and said, "You know, it's strange to me why more students don't use these books. If I were to take that test, that's what I would do." Here she bent down to the bottom shelf and brought up a book that looked like it was a ream of typing paper, held together with a binding of black duct tape. (About two inches thick)

"How much does it cost?" I asked.

"Only twenty-nine ninety-nine." she replied.

Well, in 1989, twenty-nine and change still bought a lot of burgers and shakes. "Whoa," I breathed out. "That cost might be a part of the reason so few use them. I'll take it. Cheap at any price."

The Book:

At home, the book was divided into two major parts. The first was English usage...parts of speech, tense agreement, spelling, Grammar in general. The second was an essay question giving you an opportunity to write a convincing essay, choosing from a list of four subjects. The second section was Professional Knowledge about teaching, Laws, Rulings, Opinions, etc. and then Personal knowledge about the Major Area of Study, for me of course, Music Education.

Betty and I studied that guide book like our lives both depended on it. We would go through a section, understand what we had read, and then take the test on that particular area. The part that I was weakest on was the area of Educational Law. It had been over twenty years since I had paid the least attention to any Law Enactment to do with Education, or Supreme Court decisions affecting the Teaching Profession. That part could trip me up if I didn't bone up on it more than the other parts.

The Test:

On the appointed Saturday morning I arrived at the Ed Building on the campus of EMC. It was the sight of many hours in a prior life spent listening as Dr. Gruber droned his notes to the class of insanely bored students, while occasionally glancing at the clock on the wall in the back of the room. But today was going to be different. I was loaded with a great Nightingale/Conant Positive Thinking cassette tape on the way in from Bridger. No one was going to steal this one from me. Once inside the building, in the hallway, I joined the row of anxious test takers cued for admittance into the proctored chamber of horrors. Man, oh man, you could practically smell the adrenaline oozing from every pore.

There were mostly kids who were no longer legitimately kids...mostly over twenty two who had no knowledge of the work-a-day world of adults. I decided to do my "I'm so positive, I can't even stand myself" routine. I looked at the lad standing behind me in line and I said, "Wow, I can hardly wait to get into this test. I've been studying and I am R-E-A-D-Y! You know what I mean? I mean I watch Jeopardy every day. I'm so good with questions and answers, I'm on fire. How about you?"

To which he replied, "Nice!" I ignored the look that his squinted eyes and furrowed forehead indicated.

Now turning to the cute girl in front of me I bragged, "I have all ten of my number 2 pencils sharpened to perfection. See?" I held them in my right hand for her inspection. The width of her eyes might have been a hint as to her reception of my pencil gambit. "Not a used eraser in the lot!" I continued. People were now beginning to turn toward me and glance surreptitiously in my direction. I now noticed that there was a little space developing around me. I thought, 'These folks just don't recognize Positive Mental Attitude when they see it first hand!'

This party was by invitation only. You had to have a ticket. The door opened at the front of the line and the Circus Master made his announcement, "Admittance by ticket only. Simply show me your ticket and enter the testing area. There will be exactly the number of seats required for you. Find the one you desire and be seated."

Once all the victims had been seated, the Grand Proctor made his "Testing Proctor's Statements". Your exam will be placed on your desk, face down. You may begin to fill in your vital statistics at that time. Do Not turn the test over until all have completed the front cover. At that time I will make the announcement to turn your tests over and begin. Do pay particular attention to the instructions on how to fill in the choice for your answer." Pause… "Okay, then, everyone ready? You may begin."

Lunch:

One hour for lunch...Where to eat? What about old favs? The "Milky Way" right across from the men's dorm in 1959? GONE. The Drive In just North of the school campus? A Parking lot. Sandy's across from the Billings Senior High School? Nope. The "Big Boy on Grand and 10th? Not the Big Boy any longer. How about Navasio's Slop Shop? Not there any more. That must spell an end to greasy ten cent burgers in a spotted brown paper bag. Guess I'll just settle for Tuna Fish Salad Sandwich and Coffee in the car in the parking lot.

The first part of the test had been easy. Grammar… The second part had been fun. Essay… Now came the part that I would be doing a lot of guessing on. Having been out of teaching for some ten years, my Jargon hadn't quite kept up with my "Edu-Brain". This could be tricky. A little more from Earl Nightingale's "Lead the Field" and I was ready to take on the world.

Back Home Post Exam:

Telling Betty about the experience I couldn't help but remark on what I had heard someone say about the test results and it's affect on your State Certification. In order to qualify for a teaching certificate in the State of Montana, you had to score in the 75th percentile and above. That was not the case for qualifying for a teaching position on the Native American Indian Reservation. There it was considerably lower. I wondered why that would be. It seemed to me that there was something at play that was beyond my understanding.

Do I Get To Teach Or Not:

When the results came in I was already teaching at the Roberts School on a Provisional Certificate. I'm proud to say that I had sailed through the Communication Skills portion with a high score. I also had a great score on my Major Artistic Knowledge (Music) score. My Professional Knowledge score was a little lower. That hurdle was cleared and now it was on to the challenges of setting up the new Music Department.

Summer Vacation:

As soon as the actual school year was over, I began to assess my needs as far as Pep Band was concerned. You may not realize it but the pep band is heard by the entire community. Your standing with the folks who count in your school Music program can rise or fall depending on the performance of your Pep Band. The heart of the Pep Band is the Drum Set. The heart of the Drum Set is the Drummer. Visiting with Ron, I found that the main drummer for the band had graduated that year. To the best of his ability to recall who else would be left in the drum section, Ron came up with the name Jeremy Flasky. Jeremy was a young lad that had never been given much of a chance to develop his natural abilities as a drummer because the graduated head drummer, Dennis, had been called on to play so much of the time. I got Jeremy's home phone number.

Jeremy the Drummer:

Since school had let out for the summer, the cafeteria, which was the band room, was empty for the summer. I had set out the Drum Kit near the door to my office which was a little store room at the back of the large lunch room. It, (the kit) consisted of base drum with pedal, throne, snare, two mounted tom-toms, floor tom, hi-hat and mounted cymbal. I was chatting quietly with Donna, the Secretary, while waiting for Jeremy to show up. I had asked him to bring along a pair of drum sticks just in case we wanted to bang on a drum or two. Donna said, "Mr. Brasen, have you ever met Jeremy before?"

I replied, "No. Why?"

She asked, "Are you planning on him being your main drummer for the Pep Band?"

I asked her, "Is there something I should know before I meet Jeremy?"

She said, "No. Not really. It just seems to us that he might be a little too shy to make a number one drummer."

To this I answered, "I can handle shy. I believe that shyness can be the result of not having been given enough responsibility. I can certainly change that."

About that time, in walks none other than Jeremy Flasky. Out I came from behind the office desk and shaking Jeremy's hand, I said, "Jeremy, I'm Mr. Brasen. I hope to help you become a number one drummer. Are you up for it?"

The first words I ever heard Jeremy Flasky say were, "I think so. That's what I want to be more than anything else."

Praise the Lord and pass the amunition! That was the answer I was looking for.

"Tell you what, Jeremy. Let's go into the cafeteria and go to work."

Seating him on the drummer's throne, I taught him the basic Rock Beat. "No sticks. No drums, just open palm down hands on thighs and feet on the floor. Four beats to a measure and take it slow at first. The first thing is your right foot keeps time on one, two, three and four. Now your left foot gives a little up-beat before one and three. Imagine that the right foot is your base drum and the left foot is your high-hat. Now get them to work together. Next is your left hand. Pat your left thigh with your left hand on two and four. Okay, now your right hand pats your right thigh eight times a measure. This represents your cymbal being played continuously. Practice this at home where no one can see or hear you. I believe in you. If you practice without sticks or drums as much as you can, I'll see you here in one week and we'll move on to the drum set. Now then, I see that your hands do shake a little. Is that just nerves?"

Jeremy gave a little frown, shrinking down a little and shaking his head said, "I guess!"

"Well, Jeremy, I get the shakes from nerves before I play to this very day. I count it as a good thing. It just means to me that when you are nervous and shake a little it means you want to do extra well. I'll take that every time, from everybody, in everything I do."

Jeremy sat up a little taller, straightened his shoulders, and couldn't hide a very special smile that had crept onto his lips.

I had my drummer!

7th & 8th ART APPRECIATION

Teaching at Roberts with Mr. Ron Marshall as Principal and Superintendent was fishing the Madison at Ennis, Montana, below the bridge during the Salmon Fly Hatch. Wherever you threw in your line you caught a wonderful trout. Sometimes the big lunker Brown Trout that only comes up off the bottom during the hatch would be unable to resist your line. Sometimes you could catch a nice Rainbow on a bare hook. You just had to be there at the right time and be sure your line was in the water.

When Ron and I chatted about what classes I would be teaching he mentioned that the school had been dinged for not having some form of Art Appreciation for the Junior High School students. He asked me if I could come up with a program that would satisfy that requirement. I said, "To tell you the truth, other than three quarters of Humanities in my Freshman year at E.M.C., I don't have a lot of formal training in the area but let me see what I can come up with. I'll put my thinking cap on and rummage around down in there."

What I came up with was a one year course I called "A Survey Of Popular Art". It would be divided into four separate quarterly sessions:

1. First Quarter will be Pencil Sketching 101:

In this course we will start by making sketches of examples I have in a "How to Draw" book. There are a dozen sketches from very simple to more complex. That will get us to mid-quarter. Then we'll examine the concept of fore-shortening and creating the illusion of depth on the two dimensional plane using vanishing point perspective. And finally to free hand sketching of Still Art, a display of fruit and bottles on a table top covered with checkered cloth. That would end the first quarter.

2. Second Quarter will be producing a Weekly Radio Drama 101:

For the second quarter the class would move the desks into a circle, sharing up to three on a mike, and using the stories of Classic Tales edited into all spoken lines that were in a weekly publication to which my wife Betty subscribed. I set up the tape recorder, lead the mike jacks into a mixer, sent the line out to the tape recorder and voila! We had Radio shows. They were complete with sound effects from a volume on a CD I had, or just manufactured on the spot. Did you ever crumple up a newspaper slowly up close to a microphone? You get a FIRE! I thought of having the tapes played on the school P.A. system on Friday just before the final bell of the day, but didn't get around to it.

3. Third Quarter will be Broadway Via Hollywood:

One of the areas of Popular Art that was missing in small Montana towns was the thriving Musical Comedy of New York. So I had the videos of a lot of Hollywood versions of musicals that had been adapted from the original Broadway Stage. We would start with the first major Broadway show that set the stage for most shows to follow. OKLAHOMA! We would take the better part of the week watching the show, stopping as seldom as possible to discuss items such as Character Arcs, Costuming, stage setting, language, plot and possible overall theme of the work, ending with an in class, essay on the final day describing the show based on the topics mentioned.

4. Fourth Quarter will be Producing One Act Plays including Set Design and Workshop:

Since I have long been a huge fan of the one act play, and have a minor in Educational Theater, we would be learning Set Building from flats on up, Set Construction including Set Design, Lighting Design, Painting and learn the language of Theater. While doing this we would assume roles in two separate one act plays and present them to the school for our final project.

RON'S REACTION:

Writing it up that night, I went prepared to present what I thought would be a class that even the most rustic individual would line up to take. Ron's enthusiastic response was a surprise to me. "Larry, I think this is just what the doctor ordered. How much is it going to cost the district to put this into the curriculum?"

My answer, "Very little for the most part. Some pencils and erasers and paper for the first quarter. I'll make copies of my material for handouts. I have all the equipment needed for the second quarter with the exception of some tape recorder tapes. The third quarter will be covered because I have all the DVDs we need for watching Broadway Shows. The fourth quartet will require some expenditure for wood, screws. Muslin for the flats. Paint and brushes. The plays I have in my collection of one act plays. Sooo… What do you say?"

Ron's reply said it all, "Sign me up for the class!"

CARRYING THE STORY FORWARD:

Each of the quarters have stories to be told, but I choose to tell the story of the One Act Plays. To begin with, the school had a record of producing plays with a minimum of sets, lighting, and props. So at the beginning of the Quarter of One Act Plays I ordered some pine 1 X 4 boards, a sheet of 3/8" plywood, a bunch of 5/8" phillips screws, a box of staples, (I had my own staple gun), and a partial bolt of muslin. We called a work party for all the members of the class that could attend on a Saturday morning. Ron was there to open the shop and take part in the construction of enough flats to create a set that could be used for both plays. Now that the students had a first hand knowledge of the flats, they wanted to be a part of deciding how to paint them.

The first play was a comedy about a couple of folks who were caught in an apartment on the fifth floor of a hotel with a fire beginning on the first floor. It had a lot of people stopping by to tell them the hotel was on fire and as a situation comedy, it went over very well with the class and eventually with the audience.

The second play was about an invalid lady who was confined to bed and all she had for communication was a telephone. She accidentally overheard a plot to murder an invalid in her bed, much the same as she was, through a misconnection of the telephone. She spent all the play calling for help for the lady she didn't know. No name, no address, no phone number… As the play began to climax a sound track of Igor Stravinsky's "Rites of Spring" began to play in the background at a nearly subliminal level. Second by second the Pagan Ritualistic music increased in volume, until to the utter horror of the audience and the lady alike a hunched man in a trench coat with a deadly knife raised to kill entered from the door, stage left. The only light left on the stage as he made his entry, was one flood that cast a terrifying shadow, frozen in time on the flat upstage behind him. Then at the exact moment he entered, count one, two, three...Curtain.

"AYE, THERE'S THE RUB!":

So, as the instructor, I'm watching from the audience which included the entire school that wasn't involved in the production plus thirty students from my wife, Betty's, school in Bridger, Montana. Also in the audience were many members from the community. Just as the cue was given to begin the music one of the kids came racing to me at top speed out of the door to the stage.

"Mr. B, Mr. B! George (the killer) is shaking all over and says he can't go out on the stage in front of all the people."

"Holy Moses! Okay, where is he?"

"Just right back there not far from the door for his entry."

Up I went on the stage, behind the prop tables, and sets of flats, in the semi-dark of the backstage, and there stood George. By now the music was beginning to grow louder. "George, what's the problem, my good man?"

"I just can't go out there in front of all the people!"

"I know just how you feel. I have felt the same way many times. Here let me get you a little closer to the door. I know you'll feel better than over here."

Putting my arm around him, I cajoled him into position. As the music reached it's ultimate zenith, I simply pushed George, knife and all, through the door and into Theatre History Fame.

CURTAIN!

MY FRIEND, SHELLY TURK

The year was 1989! The Music Teaching position at Roberts, Montana entailed: all Elementary General Music; Beginning, Intermediate and High School Band and Chorus; also Pep Band, Stage Band and Vocal Jazz Ensemble. Since they offered to pay me, I felt more or less obligated to fill the vacancy.

Because none of the students played piano well enough to accompany the chorus, I was constantly looking for a pianist. While reading the local want ads in the Red Lodge weekly paper, *The Carbon County News*, I stumbled on an ad for piano lessons placed by a lady living in Joliet, Montana. My phone call to her went something like this.

"Hi. Mrs. Turk, My name is Larry Brasen and I'm calling because I saw your ad in the paper."

"Oh. Were you interested in taking some private piano lessons, Mr. Brasen?"

"Well, as a matter of fact, no. However, I do have a proposition for you that I believe you will find well nigh irresistible. I teach Chorus over in Roberts and I would like to offer you the opportunity to accompany the group a couple of days a week for free. We could get you started next Tuesday or Thursday at 10:00 A.M."

Her answer surprised even me. "I'm sure I would be able to help with your situation. I do have a degree in Music Education. Could I bring my young daughter, Jenny along? She wouldn't get in the way or anything."

"You bet. I'll look forward to seeing you next Tuesday if that would be okay, and congratulations."

That was the beginning of a friendship I value to this day. Shelly and I continued our affiliation for several years. Eventually we became a real team, working together planning and teaching the chorus class while little Jenny played at her mother's feet, under the piano. The School Board finally found Shelly some travel money and later even figured out how to pay her for the time she spent playing the piano.

As I had hoped, Shelly began to work with some of my students as a private vocal coach and piano teacher. She was teaching some of the songs from *Jekyll and Hyde* which was currently playing in London. She suggested we do a presentation of the show by giving a series of musical vignettes from the play connected by a narration telling the story. It would be costumed and have a set. The students would have the opportunity to act as well as sing but it wouldn't require all the preparation a major musical would demand. Having certification in teaching educational theatre I was excited about this concept. Simple as it was, I had never thought of doing a show this way. I gave the musical direction to Shelly and I took over the dramatic needs including the construction of a rudimentary set. After weeks of intense rehearsal, the final presentation was quite well received by the Roberts audience.

There were twenty five girls in our chorus. They ranged in grade from 8th through Seniors in High School. We practiced sight singing at least ten minutes every rehearsal, studying from a sight singing course of study Shelly had discovered by attending a special music clinic for music educators which she attended and paid for out of her own pocket. As the year progressed our little chorus improved dramatically.

The District Music Festival was held in Billings towards the end of each year so we needed to pick two pieces for adjudication. We picked an English Renaissance piece by Thomas Morley that wasn't too difficult but displayed the girls intonation and diction. The second one was a piece that we both loved. It was from "The Wizard of Oz". The title was *Somewhere Over the Rainbow*. The problem with this piece is that it begins with an octave jump on the first two notes. Young choirs are notorious for either sliding all the way up to the second note or just missing it by singing the second note flat. By selecting this piece we were putting it all on the line in the first two seconds of the song. If the kids missed the second note they could do the entire remainder of the song perfectly and the best they would receive on the prepared material would be a II (Excellent) rating.

Knowing all that in advance, we worked on the first interval every rehearsal. We worked on head voice. We worked on uniform vowel formation. We worked on breath support. We worked on diaphragmatic singing. "Be like the crazy duck. Calm and peaceful on the outside but working like everything underneath."

The day of the big District Music Festival came. The kids and I boarded the bus at school and took off for Billings. Since Shelly lived in Joliet, which was on our way, we stopped there at the Log Cabin Café and picked her up. Even through her always cheerful smile, I could see she was nervous. She had invested more of herself in this group than a normal accompanist does. We were partners. The ride to Billings was uneventful. Arriving at Senior High on time, we got off the bus and reported to our assigned home room.

As the day wore on I had instrumental groups to direct also, so I only occasionally saw Shelly during most of the morning. The scores of the groups being judged were posted on a bulletin board in the main hall of the school. Out of curiosity, every time I passed that board I looked at the scores being posted by the judges for whom we were scheduled to sing later in the afternoon. They were absolutely tough. There had only been two or three "I" ratings during the entire morning. I met Shelly for lunch in the director's lounge where she reported she had been watching the judges in our room all morning and they were really good but very demanding. We knew there was nothing we could do but proceed with the program we had planned.

Meeting our girls in the home room twenty minutes before our scheduled performance, we warmed up for a few minutes, going over that octave jump at the beginning of *Over the Rainbow* several times. "Okay girls, just relax and do your very best. You'll be fine", I instructed.

Then Shelly, "Ladies, we have been working together for quite some time. You know I love you and believe in you. Like Mr. "B" says relax and enjoy."

In the hall outside the performance area we were stopped as a group. "A little delay," the guard posted at the entrance said.

"Okay, softly run the three part scale warm up." Pitch pipe to the lips, "Let's start on B-flat."

"You really shouldn't be singing out here," the guard said.

"We'll keep it soft", I whispered.

The door opened and we were ushered onto a stage with a set of choral risers in the center. A nice baby grand supplied by Eckroth Music was stage left of the group. We assembled on the risers in total silence. Glancing out at the adjudicators seated mid-auditorium at two desks propped over the seats, I noticed several parents and students from our school in attendance. There were also several students from other schools seated there. Our two stage bands and our concert band had earned "I" ratings and we had good friends in many of the other small schools. Some of these kids had come to hear our chorus perform.

To the judges, "Hi out there. How ya doin?"

"Hi. Hold on for just a minute while we finish up our paper work from the previous group. Alright?"

"No problem. Would you mind if we just did a couple warm up scales while we wait?"

"Sure, go ahead."

"Give me a C Shelly. Now, do the three part scale warm up."

After two or three scales the adjudicator said, "Okay, if you're ready, go ahead. Which one are you going to do first?"

"We're going to start with the Morley. Then we'll do *Over the Rainbow*."

Morley---Flawless!

Over the Rainbow---the opening piano and then the most perfect octave interval ever performed that day. After that it was a piece of cake.

At the end the adjudicators rose to their feet and applauded. They both were enthusiastic about our performance. The judge that approached the chorus to work with them in a special mini-seminar started with, "I was really concerned when I saw you had chosen *Over the Rainbow* to perform. That octave jump at the very beginning really separates the men from the boys. Or in your case the women from the girls. You hit it exactly. I would like to hear you do it again. Now if you want a "I" rating do it the way you did it the first time. You do want a "I", right?"

Next it was on to the sight singing room where we were greeted by another judge. As the chorus moved onto the risers an aide handed out a piece of two part vocal music totally unfamiliar to us. We had three or four minutes to look the piece over, give instructions, and begin singing. After examining the piece and talking with the chorus about it we decided to perform it with the syllable Du as opposed to using standard Solfegio (Do, Re, Mi) syllables. Shelly played the major scale in the key in which the piece was written. She was allowed to play a I, V, I in that key and we were off. The chorus sang that piece without an error. The adjudicator rose and after applauding the group told them they were one of the best groups she had heard that entire day, including groups from much larger schools than ours.

There were less than a handful of Superior (I) ratings awarded that day and we got one of them. All our hard work had paid off. On the way home that night we stopped in Laurel, Montana at the A and W Root Beer stand to enjoy a well earned reward. Boarding the bus for the rest of the ride home, the kids were unusually noisy. That is a predictable reaction to a super success such as they had experienced. Just as predictable is the lull that follows the "storm" while they quietly basked in the glow of a "Job Well Done". As Shelly rose to get off the bus at the Log Cabin Café the kids all cheered. They recognized the important part she had played in their success. Hugs, Thank yous, and High Fives saw her on her way to her car and home.

When I left Roberts, moving to Arizona, I took a part of Shelly with me. My arsenal of teaching techniques now included using vignettes of Broadway Shows and Disney type movies. In fact, my first year in Paradise Valley School System I produced "Oklahoma!" in that style.

Shelly moved on also. I believe Shelly Turk discovered how special she could be in the lives of other people while working with me and my students at

Roberts.   Shelly and her daughter Jenny went on to perform vocally with an opera company in Billings. She has also directed District Wide Youth Choirs associated with the F.F.A. group.   Later, she went on to become a very successful full time English and Computer teacher at the High School in Joliet, Montana.

I fondly think back, and wonder if my initial phone call to that unknown young piano teacher had anything to do with furthering her along her journey in the field of Education. Her success certainly makes the next phone call I need to make a little easier.

Shel Silverstein's "Skinny McGwynn"

PREP PERIODS:

What do most teachers do during their prep period? Great question. Since I was still smoking cigarettes at that time, one thing I enjoyed was befouling the air of the teacher's work room with smoke. But that could only last a little while as I drank a cup of coffee, and then what would I do? I was naturally curious about what everyone else was teaching. I loved to watch others at work. There was always stopping at the office and saying hi to Donna and checking my mailbox. Ultimately, I would wind up wandering down the Hall past the Cafeteria/Band Room on the right past my friend Georgiana's Third and Fourth Grade and finally to George's Fifth and Sixth Grade. Each one of the teachers had their special style of teaching. I admired George Nelson because of his control of the kids plus his sincere empathy for each as an individual.

On my "rounds" one day, I passed by Georgianna Marshall's Third/Fourth Grade class and I heard a student recitation. Curious, as always, (she taught with her door open) I approached. The student was reading out of a book. I really needed to know what the book was because the poems they were reading were "strange" at best. I entered the room unobserved by the students and caught a glimpse of the book title. The author was Shel

Silverstein. The name of the book was "Where the Side Walk Ends", I think. The poem was entitled "Skinny McGwynn". I had seen enough! In a flash, my mind jumped to a finished product.

THE CONCEPT:

Leaving the room, I nearly ran to the Library and my favorite Librarian, Mary Allen. "Mary, I can't believe what I just saw. The kids in Georgianna's class are reading from a book. Do you know what it is?"

Mary replied, "Larry! You look just a little frazzled. You want to sit down and take a couple of deep breaths and then start again?"

"Mary, I don't have a lot of time on this one. Some guy named Shel Silversomething. I don't know, I just have to get a copy of that book ASAP!"

Mary, calm as she always was, said, "You are going to LOVE Shel Silverstein. He makes reading actual fun. Especially for Third or Fourth Graders. You are probably referring to "Where the Sidewalk Ends". Here's a copy for you to check out."

Opening the book to the table of contents in the front I looked for "Skinny McGwynn". "Okay, here it is. I'm just gonna borrow this little baby for a while, Mary. Mark me down or whatever you have to do. I'm OUTTA HERE!!!" No longer at a mere quick step, I literally ran out of the Library, and got to my room. I still had fifteen minutes left of my prep period and I had high powered prepping to do. That very same Third/Fourth grade class was due in my room at the ringing of the very next bell.

THE ACT OF CREATION:

I picked up my trusty guitar and opening the book to the "Skinny" page, I strummed a C Chord. Here is what I found plus his very wonderful "Art Work".

SKINNY McGWYNN

Skinny McGwynn was so terribly thin
that while taking his bath Sunday night,
Out popped the plug, and
Swoosh, Slush, and Glug Glug
It washed Skinny right down that
Drain outta sight.
Where is our dear Skinny
Bathing tonight?
In some Underground Pool
Down below?
Or up there so high,
In that tub in the sky,
Where all the clean people go?
Yeah, up there so high in that tub in the sky, where all the clean people go! (My addition)

PHILOSOPHY OF ED:

Is it any wonder why the kids loved **reading** with material like that? Definitely not Spot and Jane. And that day, one of many, my kids got treated to originality in the teaching/learning relationship. Right out of their classroom, out of the book they had held in their hands just moments ago and into the dream land created by Shel Silverstein and put to music by me. Don't ya love it when stuff just comes together?

PORTFOLIO EVALUATION

It was the school year 1993-94 and I was teaching in the Roberts, Montana School System. I had attended a summer school session in Missoula that summer, adding credits for my credential renewal. In one of the classes they imported two teaching nuns from what had been a Catholic School system back East. That school had been recognized for outstanding achievement in student evaluation. Since I always seemed to have difficulty giving any student anything but an A in my music classes, I thought it might be a good idea to drop in on the class. Maybe I could pick up a concept or two to aid and abet me in my grading dilemma.

After the introduction to the class, discussion about the content, a syllabus handed out, and the class members introducing themselves, we got our first intro to the main speakers for the class. These two teachers were well organized and presented their material in orderly, understandably way. They had a Power Point presentation with charts and figures, etc. I didn't record them (I wish I had) so what follows is my interpretation/ distillation of what they said.

They discussed normal systems of grading. This involved vocabulary mastery/regurgitation. Testing hadn't yet reached it's point of dominating evaluation tactics as it has today, and yet how else was one to grade a student? For many subjects this seemed to be the most natural method to use. In Math and the Sciences it was easy to create a quiz on what had been covered in class and give a percentage grade on the answers. But they had developed an entirely new process for evaluating a student's learning in a subject area. It was called Portfolio Evaluation.

This process involved each student creating a portfolio containing his/her reactions to each class discussion, demonstration, lecture, any pertinent information about what they learned. Collect all the class notes, thoughts, information in the folder. At the end of the term, each was to prepare a presentation of what had been presented and their reaction to it. They were graded pass/fail on their projects. A copy of the portfolio was kept on file at the school and they were expected to file a copy for themselves. Imagine the power of having a copy of your ending projects in all your classes through all the years.

So, this gave me an inspiration for grading my instrumental students. This is what I did. My band students started in the 5th grade. I met with them for 30 minutes daily. One of the best beginning band schedules I could dream of. All the beginning band kids played out of the same book. On page 14 in each book was their first solo with piano accompaniment. I had each student bring in a VCR Cassette Tape labeled with their name. I had a VCR recorder donated by the Roberts Parents for the Performing Arts. Each student wore a little something extra nice for the recording. Mrs. Andrea Holman who was a math teacher, came in for the recording to play the piano. We recorded every one of the 5th grade student's first solo and kept all the tapes in a special cupboard in the band room. My intention was to create a student portfolio for each at special learning intervals in their musical progress. The idea was to give it to them as graduation presents upon Commencement from High School.

As the year zoomed along, I became aware that we, Betty and I, really wanted to move to Arizona so we could be near our son, Larry Jr. and his family which now included not only his wife, Janelle, but also our grandson Sam. As I left my music room which was built for my program for the last time, I thought wistfully about the tapes in the closet I was leaving behind. I knew they would be lost in the dust of time. It had been a great little idea at the time but now was a new day and we had new challenges to face.

Epilogue

About ten years later I visited my old school in Roberts. In chatting with someone there he said, "That was one of the most emotional graduations we've ever had. First they had the speech from the Salutatorian. Then the Valdevictorian gave her talk. That was followed by the main speaker they brought in from Billings. And then, before awarding the diplomas, they announced a special visit from some old friends they hadn't seen in years. They played the tapes of each of those little kids playing their first solos that you recorded. Lord! There wasn't a dry eye in the house."

<u>*Conclusion*</u>

If a person had a portfolio of where he/she came from to where they are today and played it for themselves just before an important event in their life can you imagine the incredible boost to self image that could be?

PORTFOLIO EVALUATION!!!

A Renaissance Christmas Program

The Concept:

To start out I must tell you that in my third or fourth year in Roberts I went insane for the Christmas Program. I tired of calling it the Winter Program, the First Semester Fling, the End of the Year Celebration, etc. Let's just do it as a Christmas Show. I mean, it's a small community with a lot of similar folks making it up. Who's gonna care if we really do a Christmas Show? We'll have students take turns reading the Christmas Story out of the King James Bible. Starting with the annunciation through the birth of Jesus.

Since the King James version of the Bible was written in the English of the time, not unlike Shakespeare might have used in his high dramas, I realized that I could make this a Renaissance Christmas. We could include the work of several of the famous artists of the time, depicting the Christmas Story in Renaissance written work (the Bible), vocal music(Christmas Carols) and art (European Masters) of the time.

Approval:

I knew that there could be some possible backlash from some of the community, so I took it to Mr. Marshall for his approval. "A Renaissance Christmas!

Who would have thought of that? You bet! Sounds like a great idea!"

Implementation:

I went to my good friend, Mary the librarian, and engaged her in my plan. Her job, if she accepted it would be to obtain slides of the great works of art showing the Christmas Story. She said, "Can do!", readily agreed to this idea and went to work. Also, we would need a projector that was bright enough to see the pictures in the gym. I next asked my shop teacher, Jerry, if he could make a frame for a screen, ten foot square, and then staple muslin to it and paint it white and figure out how to suspend it over the students on the choral risers. He said, "If it's possible, consider 'er done."

Performance:

Thursday night before the Christmas Break...a packed gym...nearly every kid in the school was in the big program. First the Grade school kids did their thing. Audience very polite...(Who doesn't love the little ones?) Then Beginning Band. Okay, a few clinkers here and there but recognizable tunes played by novice musicians. Then High School Band (7th and 8th) included. Warm reception. I don't think the band ever sounded better. Then the Stage Band...Just absolutely HOT!!! My Word!!! And then the chorus took the risers. House lights down...

I made an announcement that went something like this, "Ladies and Gentlemen, what you have witnessed so far this evening is a sharing of talents relaying the Commercial and Folksie side of the season. What you are about to experience is a combination of the work of several instructors here together with me and my students to create a little different kind of Christmas Program. We've attempted to create a Renaissance Christmas...including songs written roughly around the time of the Renaissance, images created during that time by European artistic masters and the spoken word out of the King James Bible written in that day. This is an artistic telling of the story of the birth of Jesus. Please consider this our Christmas Gift to you in this Season."

With that the lights went totally down (only exit lights showing) and the first slide went up on the big screen above the chorus. The defused light from the screen dimly lit the faces of the chorus members as they started their first song… With every slide there came a soft murmur from the crowd the chorus singing the appropriate carol.

Finally, we all sang "Silent Night" together with the massed Band and Chorus and audience.

Lights up. Concert over. Standing ovation. Ahhh!!!

The general comment went something like this, "This is what a real Christmas Program should look like."

It is probably the last program of its kind that will ever be shown in our little school gym. It only takes one person to come to the Superintendent and complain about "Separation of Church and State" to make one stop and think of the possible consequences of their actions.

When Ron came to me later and explained that had happened, I said to him, "Well, my friend. We had a heck of final Christmas Show didn't we? I guess that next year we'll be back to "The Winter Festival". And that's okay too."

Roberts Stage Band (Part 1)

<u>BEGINNINGS:</u>

From the start I knew I wanted, more than anything, a real Kick Butt Stage Band. A stage band is comprised as a rule of Saxophones, one Bari, two Altos, and two Tenors, four Trumpets, four Bones, Piano, Guitar, Bass, assorted Percussion including the Drum Set. I bought a complete set of Beginning Stage Band books. There were twelve songs in the book and I think they were arranged by Sammy Nestico. He arranges so even a small group gets a full sound and really Swings.

In the second week of school I had the beginning seeds of a Stage Band Selected. A talented Senior boy named Mark Wright played Alto Sax. He and I conferred on the likely members of the group. After seeking them out one at a time, we decided we would meet in the band room one hour before school started on a Tuesday morning. At that meeting before getting instruments out I had everyone take their book and look at the first tune we would play. I seem to remember it being "CUTE" by Nestico. "Just listen and get the feel of the music. Watch the music like you are playing it on your instrument."

With Mark helping with the reeds and me with the brass we were beginning to sound. Putting it together, hey! Not bad for the first time. The piece "CUTE" has a lot of spaces for drum fills. Jeremy wasn't quite ready for the swing fills. He did his best and even though it sounded a little like someone throwing rocks at the snare, as we worked through it he got better on the spot.

Stage Band's First Public Performance:

I am a firm believer in performance based musical learning. I want to have a public performance for every group as a culminating experience every quarter. A quarter is just about the perfect length of time to make a noticeable difference in a person's skills. It also sets an expectation on the part of the students that they have a deadline to meet. Nothing drives a person like a GOAL that has a deadline.

Stage Band started meeting before school on Tuesdays and Thursdays. Downbeat was forty five minutes before the Homeroom bell. We prepared three pieces for that first concert. Swing one piece, Rock one piece, and Latin one piece… Wow!!! They were already HOT!!!

Year's End, First Year:

By the end of the first year we entered the Stage Band in the District Music Festival. We did very well. We earned and received a II rating. Of course, I wanted a I but there is nothing wrong with a II. (Well, that's not quite right. Whats wrong is it's not a I.) But for a first year group it was respectable. I noticed that there were III ratings posted.

It was here that I got the chance to meet a new friend, Todd Nass, the band director from Absarokee School. Absarokee is a much larger school district than Roberts. I noticed his Stage Band received a I rating. Todd looked for me at the director's meeting and introduced himself. He was interested in the fact that I had started a Stage Band in Roberts. He wanted to hear all about the experience I was having.

By the end of the year, we may not have been kicking butt, however we had made tremendous progress. We graduated some valuable members as Seniors that Spring. Mark on Lead Alto and Johna Mathes on Bari Sax as well as others. But I knew in advance and so planned on their replacements.

Year Start, Second Year:

The Stage Band started meeting from six PM to 8 PM on Tuesday nights. My plan of action for the group was to have twelve pieces ready by the end of the first quarter. We worked on one Jazz/Swing piece, one Rock piece and one Latin/Bossa piece each meeting along with reviewing everything we already had worked out. We also worked on the "Blues Scale" as a band in five keys most common to band instruments. With everyone knowing that scale, I could give anyone a solo on the spot and using that scale they could improvise a solo.

Todd's Idea:

After Basketball season, during the preparation for Honor Band practices Todd Nass and I had a rather interesting conversation. "Larry, how is your Stage Band coming along? Would they be ready to play for a dance?"

Replying, I said, "Well, we have a good number of pieces ready, but how long would the dance be? And why do you ask?"

Todd confided in me, "My kids in Stage Band and I want to hold a Dance. The problem is we don't have enough numbers to play for two hours. My idea is, if you're ready, we could each do half the dance. Maybe we could end the show with a couple of combined numbers...a real big band sound. What do you think?"

My experience with music directors in schools has been that they tend to be a little defensive about what they do and how they do it. This opportunity was so open and assumed so much that was positive that it kind of knocked me off my feet. I had nothing to conceal from Todd and he had nothing to worry about from me. I couldn't help my mouth forming a little grin. I had never met anyone like Todd in my professional career and was pleased with what I saw.

"I would love to. I'll have to talk it over with my Super, Ron, and we would need to set a date."

Todd smiled, "Oh, I already have the date and the time and the place. I just knew you would be ready to do it."

Meet the Competition:

I should mention at this point in this tale that Absarokee was the largest school in our sporting district. The competition between our school and theirs had always been fierce. All the kids in both schools could identify the other's coaches and players. Coach Al and Coach Ron (my boss) were notorious competitors and nobody hated to lose more than they or their team members. Knowing this in advance, made me a little leery about broaching the subject to my Stage Band.

I first brought the subject up with Ron. I was mildly surprised at his comment, "Well, Larry. You know that there is a real sense of competitiveness between our schools. I just would hate to see our kids put down by competing with that school. Do you think they are up to it?"

"Oh, yah. I'm sure they're up to it, I said while momentarily allowing the possible negative to creep in. But when I told the band about it, they were excited. Nothing makes all the practice gel like setting a date.

The Dance:

Less than a month later, we took twenty pieces to the old Absarokee gym for the dance. Absarokee took the first forty five minutes. They were just as good as I knew they would be. I hoped that having to listen to that group didn't have the city mouse/country mouse affect on my kids. It took about fifteen minutes to set up for the second half of the dance. I told the kids, "Now, after we're tuned up and ready to start the first tune, I want you to hit the very first note that we play really big. Just **blow them away!!!**" And they did. I don't believe I had ever heard them play that well.

Ride Home:

After everything was over and we were all on the bus and ready to head home, the students were all talking with each other like a *Murder of Crows* after one is shot and falls on the ground. I got on the bus with Betty and yelled out, "Okay everyone, I'd like to say something before we start home. I'm so proud of you. You really did the job tonight. Congratulations!"

At this point one of my girl leads, Mykel Mathews, lead Alto said, "**Hell**, Mr. B! We just kicked **Major Butt!** And it was **Absarokee!**" I swear I saw tears rolling down her cheeks. Oh My Goodness! What a Joy! What a ride home!

Roberts Stage Band Part 2

I had the opportunity to teach with Ron and the assembled group of real pros for five years. As you can tell if you've been reading these tales of ours they were some of the most positive and pleasurable teaching times of my life. There was very little disharmony within the staff, administration, community and student body. When you're working in that kind of atmosphere, it allows your creative side to really blossom. In those five years I had only a couple of rough spots. One concerned a student in Stage Band. She was our lead Tenor Sax player. As I remember it, I believe it was in my third year there.

THE RULE:

I had made a written rule that each member was allowed to miss up to two unexcused Stage Band rehearsals in a year. Of course that didn't count sickness or other excused absences. Our First Chair Tenor Sax player had already taken two such unexcused absences when in the third quarter (Winter) we were at our evening rehearsal when I noticed that she was missing. I had seen her just minutes before, talking with her boyfriend in the hall, and mentioned that she should come into the rehearsal right away. That she already had two absences and she knew the rule. I told her, "You know I love you as if you were my own daughter, but the rule applies to everyone equally. Please don't make this mistake."

With that I moved another Tenor player up to Second Chair and Second Chair up to First. At the break half way through rehearsal I looked in the school for her. Nothing to be seen. At the end, the Tenor that got promoted to First Chair asked, "Am I going to be playing First Tenor from now on?"

I replied, "For right now, yes. If you need to, take the folder home and practice for the next rehearsal. I'm not sure what happened to her. I'll find out. She already had two unexcused misses. We'll see!" As she picked up her folder and instrument and headed for the door I overheard her say, under her breath, "I'll bet she's back in next week."

WHAT IS BEST FOR ALL:

The next day I went directly to Ron's (my boss) office before school and explained what had happened the previous night. "I'm afraid I'm in a bit of a hard spot, boss," I showed him in writing the rule I had made. "I gave her every chance to come into the practice. She was at school. I'm sure her parents thought she was under my care. I just want you to be aware of what is going on in the event of anything coming from this. I'm going to see if I can find her now and let her know she's out for the remainder of the year."

Ron said, "Larry, are you sure there is no other way of handling this? Maybe a temporary suspension? Anything?"

"I can't see it." I left his office feeling about as low as a snail's pseudopod.

I found her by her locker. "I need to have a serious chat with you about last night."

She said, "I'm not really out am I?"

"Let's find a spot to talk privately," I said.

"I'm out. I knew it. I can't believe, I'm out. Can I have my dad come and talk to you about it with Mr. Marshall?"

"Sure. Of course you can. But I don't think it'll do any good as far as you being out of the group for the rest of the year."

Tears forming in her eyes, a little quivering of the chin, head bowed down and then back up, tears openly running down her cheeks, she said, "I love you Mr. Brasen. I just wish I had listened to you last night...."

Before she could say the rest of her plea, I interrupted, "My dear friend, school is starting, we both have to get to class." With that I hurried to my first class of the day.

Before fifteen minutes had elapsed my friend and co-worker , Mrs. Holmen. appeared at my door. "Pardon me Mr. Brasen, but Mr. Marshall sent me here to watch your class while you have a chat with him and a parent." Of course I knew that she had phoned her folks and asked for "Divine Intervention" with the Boss. I knew it was going to be an important conference. I felt as though I was ready for it. I knew how much of the full program was hanging in the balance if I backed down from my stance at that point. I marched to the office.

Mr. Marshall and the girl's dad chatted with me for about twenty minutes. Each time her father offered a compromise it ended with me saying that as much as I hated to have her miss the remainder of the year, I had the rest of the students and the rest of her life to be concerned about. That she should know that her dad had tried his very best to support her even though she was in the wrong. That proved that he loved her and I proved I loved her long term.

Even though I felt awful at the time about the situation, in retrospect, I'll have to say that attendance at rehearsals was not a problem after that. In fact, I don't believe we had another unexcused absence in the last two and a half years of my time teaching there. By the way, she came back the next year and was lead Tenor for the rest of my stay at Roberts. A totally dedicated student.

STAGE-BAND-A-RAMA:

I dream up my best new ideas at the time just before I wake up all the way in the morning. I start to wake up, I close my eyes tightly so no light can get in, I start to try to make myself aware of my own breathing, counting the inhalation as one and then the expulsion of air through pursed lips on 2, 3, 4, 5. As I do that exercise I seldom get far beyond 5 or 6 before I drift into some kind of dreamlike state where ideas "POP" up. Sometimes the ideas are just awful. I discard them and go back to the counting of breaths. If I have been working during the preceding day on any project that requires inventive thinking, a lot of the time solutions will come to me out of the blue during that exercise. I don't know how to explain it any differently than to describe the routine I follow.

In my last year at Roberts I spent a lot of time thinking of how to promote the Stage Band. I thought a lot of how Todd Nass had invited our Stage Band over to Absarokee and the positive effect it had on my entire program.   I awoke one morning in January with a solution in my brain. It was wholly formed in all the beauty of organized thought.

THE IDEA:

Stage-Band-Arama, an over dose of stage band music from four different schools, was an idea that grew from Todd's brain to mine. A stage band in each corner of the gym in Roberts, with each taking fifteen minute turns to play three of four pieces and then handing it off to the next one in line. But who to invite? Well, number one, what schools in the nearby vicinity had stage bands to begin with?

Of course the closest school was either Joliet or Bridger. Neither of them had stage bands. Of course

Absarokee, although further away, we had been over to their Stage Band Dance and so we were excited to invite them to our program in return. The second school was Red Lodge. It was a class B school, much larger than any of our C schools. I knew the director quite well. I knew his band also and it was good. Greg would come I was sure. Fromberg didn't have a stage band. Belfry...I knew the director there also and he was working on his ensemble program. Maybe he would have something he could offer. Upon giving him a call he said, "You bet! I could put an ensemble together that could play a while.

I said to him, "How about thirty minutes? Could you get a group to do two fifteen minutes slots?" He answered that he could if he had about a month to work on it. I told him that I was planning the program for the end of February or the middle of March, just after the State Basketball Tournament. He said it was a done deal.

THE ROBERTS PARENTS FOR THE PERFORMING ARTS:

From the very beginning of my tenure at Roberts I knew the value of having a parent support group. I learned that from my friend Noel Collins when I took over the music job at Joliet, Montana after returning from three years in the United States Virgin Islands, on Saint Thomas. Noel's parent group which I inherited was named <u>The Parents of Note.</u> After calling a couple of meetings with my new parents at Roberts we decided to call our group <u>The Roberts Parents for the Performing</u>

<u>Arts.</u> Most of the money they made from pizza sales and other fund raisers went to pay for student's tuitions for summer camps. They jumped on board the Stage-Band-A-Rama with all their feet. They helped with advertising, logistics, just being there and setting up a snack bar as a fund raiser. So… all was set for the big night!

THE BIG NIGHT:

All four bands were present. The parking lot was full of cars, foreign and domestic. The bleachers were loaded and the gym floor was simply a mess. People spilled out into the entryway and up into the office entrance. The RPPA (my parent group), was present and had helped with any set up procedures where they were needed. And they had their snack bar in the Library all set and going. Each of the bands was extremely well rehearsed and played their hearts out. Belfry was the smallest group but Boy did they sound great. Todd's group from Absarokee were upbeat and featured more ad lib solos than any of the other groups. Red Lodge reflected their director, Greg, in that every single note was perfectly timed and in tune. Our band was the largest there. As you can see from the picture I've included we had considerably more than the normal sixteen to eighteen members. In fact we had two stage bands that we combined together. One was made up of only High School students and the other had Junior High students in it too.

It was our turn to play our second set. I had saved the girls, Cassie and Annie, as a special for the middle of our set. I knew that none of the other schools had anything that could compare to them. Theirs is a special story I'm writing next…

I saved for our last number the special arrangement of Manhattan Transfer's performance piece "Birdland". There is a solo section that can be repeated as many times as one wishes. We made it last so that anyone who wanted could solo based on the pentatonic scale. The kids all knew that scale in the five main keys used for stage bands. We ended the show to tremendous applause from bands and audience.

The Parents For The Performing Arts made enough to send any of our kids to Summer Music Camp that wanted to go.

To wind up the year the Stage Band which included the Seventh and Eighth Graders received a I rating at the District festival. Because of the presence of pre-high schoolers they weren't allowed to go on to State.

The High School Stage Band also received a I rating and went on to State and received a I rating there. That year the state was divided into East and West Montana. We were at Billings where only three Stage bands were awarded I ratings.

UNFORGETTABLE BAND MEMBERS 1994

ANNIE AND CASSIE

OH, MY LOVE:

With the four bands committed to the Band-A-Rama, we were off and running. It was about this time that two beautiful young seventh grade girls came to me and asked if I would listen to them sing a song they had been working on. Of course I said, "Sure, when would you like to sing for me?"

Cassie said, "Could we do it when no other kids would be around? We don't want anyone to hear us but you."

A couple days later just after school let out we met in the band room. "Well, girls, what tune did you decide to sing?"

Annie replied, "Do you know a song called Unchained Melody?"

"Oh, sure," I replied. "Righteous Brothers, right?"

"We don't know about that, we just really love this song."

"Well, do you have some kind of accompaniment record or something to sing to?"

Cassie and Annie both responded together, "We just sing it with nothing."

"Well, then, let's hear what you've got!"

Settling down in my chair, I wasn't really ready for what came next. After one of them giving a pitch on the piano, I heard one of the cleanest, clearest soprano voices in the world start, "Oh, my love, my darling…" I was swept off my chair. The other took a turn. Same gorgeous tone quality, same reaction from me. Then came the bridge… "Lonely rivers flow, (echoing lonely rivers flow…) together intertwining as one voice… harmonizing… in perfect pitches… sweet, innocent, and captivating.

When they got done, "What did you think, Mr. B? Okay?"

"Girls, that is beautiful. Tell you what. Just the way you have it… no accompaniment… acapella… I'm going to schedule you during the Stage-Band-Arama at the end of February or early March. You two practice just the way you did it right here and you'll be on. That was one of the most beautiful duets I've ever heard."

THE BIG NIGHT:

It was the Stage Band's turn to play our second set. This was to be the time for Cassie and Annie to sing their Unchained Melody. During our down time just before we played the last set, the girls came to me in private in the Band Room and confessed that they were too nervous to sing. They were both shaking like Quaker Aspen in a gale. You could see the movement across the hall. Here is what I told them. I had it told to me by my director, Mr. Arthur Brandvold, when I was their age. "You have to take your eyes off of yourself and put them on the people you're performing for. You must understand that you have a gift to give them. It is a special gift that NO ONE ELSE ON EARTH HAS TO SHARE! Concentrate on THEM. The only thing you need to remember is to BREATHE DEEP and SING so you can share your gift with the folks. I'll get everyone quiet. Then you take over the job and give it your best."

We played the first song of our last set and then it came time to introduce Cassie and Annie. "Ladies and gentlemen! May I have your attention." That was followed by some subsiding of the general chatter and noise of a huge group of people—some getting ready to go—packing instruments—talking with new friends made at the event—we needed total silence. "Ladies and gentlemen, students, everyone," at the top of the public address system, the group got quiet. "Introducing Annie and Cassie to perform Unchained Melody. Ladies, the floor is all yours."

They took their mikes and stepped out in front of the band. Then that gorgeous Soprano voice started, "Oh, my love…" once again having that quieting affect on the crowd. By the the time the second voice joined in the audience was in their hands. In all the world the only thing that could be heard right at that time was their music.

<u>*ASSESSMENT:*</u>

Later in the band room again, "How did we do Mr. B?"

"A couple of things… did you notice how once you started to sing you could hear a pin drop. I mean even people in the hall got quiet and were transported by your voices. More important, how did **you** think you did?"

"It really worked, Mr. B. All my nerves went away and it was like magic."

"It always does when you give honestly of yourself to your audience."